CULTURE AND VALUE

CULTURE AND VALUE

Ludwig Wittgenstein

Edited by
G. H. VON WRIGHT

in collaboration with
HEIKKI NYMAN

Translated by
PETER WINCH

The University of Chicago Press

The University of Chicago Press, Chicago 60637
Basil Blackwell, Oxford

English translation © 1980 by Basil Blackwell
First published in 1977 as *Vermischte Bemerkungen*
© 1977 by Suhrkamp Verlag, Frankfurt am Main
All rights reserved

English-language edition published 1980

Printed in Great Britain

Library of Congress Cataloging in Publication Data

Wittgenstein, Ludwig, 1889–1951.
   Culture and value.

   Translation of Vermischte Bemerkungen.
   Includes index.
   1. Philosophy—Collected works.   I.   Wright,
Georg Henrik von, 1916-   II.   Title.
B3376.W561W7413   192   80–15234
ISBN 0–226–90432–6

VORWORT

Im handschriftlichen Nachlaß von Wittgenstein kommen häufig Aufzeichnungen vor, die nicht unmittelbar zu den philosophischen Werken gehören, obgleich sie unter den philosophischen Texten zerstreut sind. Diese Aufzeichnungen sind teils autobiographisch, teils betreffen sie die Natur der philosophischen Tätigkeit, teils handeln sie von Gegenständen allgemeiner Art wie z. B. von Fragen der Kunst oder der Religion. Sie vom philosophischen Text scharf zu trennen ist nicht immer möglich; in vielen Fällen hat Wittgenstein jedoch selbst eine solche Trennung angedeutet – durch den Gebrauch von Parenthesen oder auf andere Weise.

Einige dieser Aufzeichnungen sind ephemär, andere jedoch – die Mehrzahl – von großem Interesse. Manchmal sind sie von augenfälliger Schönheit und Tiefe. Es war den Nachlaßverwaltern klar, daß eine Anzahl dieser Aufzeichnungen veröffentlicht werden müßte. G. H. von Wright wurde beauftragt, eine Auslese vorzunehmen und zusammenzustellen.

Die Aufgabe war recht schwierig; zu verschiedenen Zeiten machte ich mir verschiedene Vorstellungen davon, wie sie am besten zu bewältigen wäre. So z. B. stellte ich mir anfangs vor, man könne die Bemerkungen nach den behandelten Gegenständen gruppieren – etwa »Musik«, »Architektur«, »Shakespeare«, »Aphorismen zur Lebensweisheit«, »Philosophie«, u. dgl. Manchmal sind die Bemerkungen ohne Zwang in solche Gruppen einreihbar, aber im Ganzen würde eine derartige Aufspaltung des Materials wohl künstlich wirken. Ich hatte ferner einmal gedacht, auch bereits Gedrucktes mitaufzunehmen. Viele der eindrucksvollsten »Aphorismen« Wittgensteins findet man ja in den philosophischen Werken – in den Tagebüchern aus dem ersten Weltkrieg, im *Tractatus*, und auch in den *Untersuchungen*. Ich möchte sagen: inmitten dieser Kontexte üben die Aphorismen Wittgensteins tatsächlich ihre stärkste Wirkung aus. Aber eben darum schien es mir nicht richtig, sie aus ihrem Zusammenhang zu reißen.

Auch hatte mir einmal vorgeschwebt, die Auswahl nicht allzu umfangreich zu machen, sondern nur die »besten« Bemerkungen aufzunehmen. Eine große Materialmenge würde, wie ich meinte, den Eindruck der guten Bemerkungen nur schwächen. *Das* ist wohl richtig – aber meine Aufgabe war nicht die eines Geschmacksrichters. Auch habe ich mir im allgemeinen nicht zugetraut, zwischen wiederholten Formulierungen desselben oder fast desselben Gedankens eine Wahl zu treffen. Selbst die Wiederholungen kamen mir oft als zur Sache gehörig vor.

Am Ende habe ich mich für dasjenige Ausleseprinzip entschieden, das mir als einziges unbedingt richtig vorkam. Ich ließ die Aufzeichnungen rein »persönlicher« Art aus der Sammlung weg – d. h. Aufzeichnungen, in denen Wittgenstein über seine äußeren Lebensumstände, seine Gemütsverfassung

PREFACE

In the manuscript material left by Wittgenstein there are numerous notes which do not belong directly with his philosophical works although they are scattered amongst the philosophical texts. Some of these notes are auto-biographical, some are about the nature of philosophical activity, and some concern subjects of a general sort, such as questions about art or about religion. It is not always possible to separate them sharply from the philosophical text; in many cases, however, Wittgenstein himself hinted at such a separation – by the use of brackets or in other ways.

Some of these notes are ephemeral; others on the other hand – the majority – are of great interest. Sometimes they are strikingly beautiful and profound. It was evident to the literary executors that a number of these notes would have to be published. G. H. von Wright was commissioned to make a selection and arrange it.

It was a decidedly difficult task; at various times I had different ideas about how best to accomplish it. To begin with, for example, I imagined that the remarks could be arranged according to the topics of which they treated – such as "music", "architecture", "Shakespeare", "aphorisms of practical wisdom", "philosophy", and the like. Sometimes the remarks can be arranged into such groupings without strain, but by and large, splitting up the material in this way would probably give an impression of artificiality. At one time moreover I had thought of including already published material. For many of Wittgenstein's most impressive "aphorisms" are to be found in his philosophical works – in the *Notebooks* from the First World War, in the *Tractatus*, and in the *Investigations* too. I should like to say that it is when they are embedded in such contexts that Wittgenstein's aphorisms really have their most powerful effect. But for that very reason it did not seem to me right to tear them from their surroundings.

At one time too I played with the idea of not making a very extensive selection, but including only the "best" remarks. The impression made by the good remarks would, I thought, only be weakened by a great mass of material. *That*, presumably, is true – but it was not my job to be an arbiter of taste. Furthermore, I did not trust myself to choose between repeated formulations of the same, or nearly the same, thought. Often the repetitions themselves seem to me to have a substantial point.

In the end I decided on the only principle of selection that seemed to me unconditionally right. I excluded from the collection notes of a purely "personal" sort – i.e. notes in which Wittgenstein is commenting on the external circumstances of his life, his state of mind and relations with other people – some of whom are still living. Generally speaking these notes were *easy* to separate from the rest and they are on a *different* level of interest from

und Beziehungen zu anderen, zum Teil noch lebenden Personen berichtet. Diese Aufzeichnungen waren von den übrigen im allgemeinen *leicht* zu trennen und ihr Interesse liegt auf einer *anderen* Ebene als das der hier gedruckten. Nur in einigen wenigen Fällen, wo diese beiden Bedingungen nicht erfüllt erschienen, habe ich auch solche Notizen autobiographischer Art aufgenommen.

Die Bemerkungen erscheinen hier in chronologischer Ordnung mit Angabe des Jahres, dem sie entstammen. Es muß auffallen, daß beinahe die Hälfte der Bemerkungen aus der Zeit nach dem Abschluß (1945) des ersten Teils der *Philosophischen Untersuchungen* stammt.

Einem Leser, der nicht mit den Lebensumständen oder mit der Lektüre Wittgensteins vertraut ist, werden manche der Bemerkungen ohne eine nähere Erklärung dunkel oder rätselhaft vorkommen. In vielen Fällen wäre es denn auch möglich gewesen, Erklärungen durch kommentierende Fußnoten zu geben. Mit ganz wenigen Ausnahmen jedoch habe ich auf Kommentare verzichtet. Sei es nebenbei bemerkt, daß *alle* Fußnoten vom Herausgeber herrühren.

Es ist unvermeidlich, daß ein Buch wie dieses auch in die Hände von Lesern gerät, denen das philosophische Werk Wittgensteins sonst unbekannt ist und auch bleiben wird. Das muß nicht unbedingt schädlich oder nutzlos sein. Es ist indessen meine Überzeugung, daß man diese Aufzeichnungen nur gegen den Hintergrund von Wittgensteins Philosophie richtig verstehen und schätzen kann und darüber hinaus, daß sie zum Verständnis dieser Philosophie beitragen.

Die Auswahl der Bemerkungen aus den Handschriften wurde in den Jahren 1965–1966 vorgenommen. Dann habe ich die Arbeit bis zum Jahre 1974 liegenlassen. Bei der schließlichen Auslese und Zusammenstellung der Sammlung hat mir Herr Heikki Nyman geholfen. Er hat auch die genaue Übereinstimmung der Textstellen mit den Handschriften kontrolliert und manche Fehler und Lücken meines Typoskripts beseitigt. Ich bin ihm für seine mit großer Sorgfalt und gutem Geschmack ausgeführte Arbeit sehr dankbar; ohne diese Hilfe hätte ich mich wahrscheinlich nie entschließen können, die Sammlung für den Druck fertigzustellen. Auch Herrn Rush Rhees schulde ich tiefen Dank für Korrekturen in dem hergestellten Text und für wertvolle Ratschläge bei der Auswahl.

Helsinki, im Januar 1977   Georg Henrik von Wright

those which are printed here. Only in a few cases where these two conditions seemed not to be met did I include notes of an autobiographical nature as well.

The remarks are published here in chronological order with an indication of their year of origin. It is conspicuous that nearly half the remarks stem from the period after the completion (in 1945) of Part One of *Philosophical Investigations*.

In the absence of further explanation some of the remarks will be obscure or enigmatic to a reader who is not familiar with the circumstances of Wittgenstein's life or with what he was reading. In many cases it would have been possible to provide explanatory comments in footnotes. I have nevertheless, with very few exceptions, refrained from adding comments. I ought to add that all the footnotes are the editor's.[1]

It is unavoidable that a book of this sort will reach the hands of readers to whom otherwise Wittgenstein's philosophical work is, and will remain, unknown. This need not necessarily be harmful or useless. I am all the same convinced that these notes can be properly understood and appreciated only against the background of Wittgenstein's philosophy and, furthermore, that they make a contribution to our understanding of that philosophy.

I began making my selection from the manuscripts in the years 1965–1966. I then laid the work aside until 1974. Mr. Heikki Nyman helped me with the final selection and arrangement of the collection. He also checked that the text agreed exactly with the manuscripts and removed many errors and gaps from my typescript. I am very grateful to him for his work, which he carried out with great care and good taste. Without his help I should probably not have been able to bring myself to complete the collection for the press. I am also deeply indebted to Mr. Rush Rhees for making corrections in the text which I produced and for giving me valuable advice on matters of selection.

Helsinki, January 1977   Georg Henrik von Wright

---

[1] A few footnotes have been added by the translator. These are indicated, like this one:
(Tr.).

VORWORT ZUR ZWEITEN AUSGABE

Diese Neuausgabe der »Vermischten Bemerkungen« enthält zusätzliches Material, zum größten Teil aus einem Notizbuch, das wahrscheinlich aus dem Jahr 1944 stammt.

Helsinki, im Juni 1978   G. H. v. W.

PREFACE TO THE SECOND EDITION

This new edition of *"Vermischte Bemerkungen"*[1] contains additional material, mainly from a notebook which probably dates from 1944.

Helsinki, June 1978   G. H. v. W.

TRANSLATOR'S ACKNOWLEDGMENTS

Many people have given me generous help with this translation. I want especially to mention Miss Marina Barabas, Messrs. S. Ellis and Heikki Nyman, Professors Steven Burns, Stephan Körner, Norman Malcolm and G. H. von Wright, Miss Helen Widdess and Mrs. Erika Winch.

But I most particularly want to thank Mr. Rush Rhees whose help and advice, on many different matters, have been quite extraordinarily valuable.

King's College, London,   Peter Winch
November 1979

---

[1] *"Vermischte Bemerkungen"*, literally translated as "Miscellaneous Remarks", is here published in English translation under the title *"Culture and Value"*. (Tr.)

VERMISCHTE BEMERKUNGEN

1914

Wenn wir einen Chinesen hören, so sind wir geneigt, sein Sprechen für ein unartikuliertes Gurgeln zu halten. Einer, der chinesisch versteht, wird darin die *Sprache* erkennen. So kann ich oft nicht den *Menschen* im Menschen erkennen.

1929

Meine Art des Philosophierens ist mir selbst immer noch, und immer wieder, neu, und daher muß ich mich so oft wiederholen. Einer anderen Generation wird sie in Fleisch und Blut übergegangen sein, und sie wird die Wiederholungen langweilig finden. Für mich sind sie notwendig.

Es ist gut, daß ich mich nicht beeinflussen lasse!

Ein gutes Gleichnis erfrischt den Verstand.

Es ist schwer einem Kurzsichtigen einen Weg zu beschreiben. Weil man ihm nicht sagen kann: »schau auf den Kirchturm dort 10 Meilen von uns und geh' in dieser Richtung.«

In keiner religiösen Konfession ist soviel durch den Mißbrauch metaphysischer Ausdrücke gesündigt worden, wie in der Mathematik.

Der menschliche Blick hat es an sich, daß er die Dinge kostbar machen kann, allerdings werden sie dann auch teurer.

Laß nur die Natur sprechen und über der Natur kenne nur *ein* höheres, aber nicht das, was die anderen denken könnten.

Die Tragödie besteht darin, daß sich der Baum nicht biegt, sondern bricht. Die Tragödie ist etwas unjüdisches. Mendelssohn ist wohl der untragischste Komponist.

CULTURE AND VALUE

1914

We tend to take the speech of a Chinese for inarticulate gurgling. Someone who understands Chinese will recognize *language* in what he hears. Similarly I often cannot discern the *humanity* in a man.

1929

I still find my own way of philosophizing new, and it keeps striking me so afresh; that is why I need to repeat myself so often. It will have become second nature to a new generation, to whom the repetitions will be boring. I find them necessary.

It's a good thing I don't allow myself to be influenced!

A good simile refreshes the intellect.

It is difficult to tell a short-sighted man how to get somewhere. Because you cannot say to him: "Look at that church tower ten miles away and go in that direction."

There is no religious denomination in which the misuse of metaphysical expressions has been responsible for so much sin as it has in mathematics.

The human gaze has a power of conferring value on things; but it makes them cost more too.

Just let nature speak and acknowledge only *one* thing as higher than nature, but not what others may think.

You get tragedy where the tree, instead of bending, breaks. Tragedy is something un-Jewish. Mendelssohn is, I suppose, the most untragic of composers.

Jeden Morgen muß man wieder durch das tote Gerölle dringen, um zum lebendigen, warmen Kern zu kommen.

Ein neues Wort ist wie ein frischer Same, der in den Boden der Diskussion geworfen wird.

Mit dem vollen philosophischen Rucksack kann ich nur langsam den Berg der Mathematik steigen.

Mendelssohn ist nicht eine Spitze, sondern eine Hochebene. Das englische an ihm.

Niemand kann einen Gedanken für mich denken, wie mir niemand als ich den Hut aufsetzen kann.

Wer ein Kind mit Verständnis schreien hört, der wird wissen, daß andere seelische Kräfte, furchtbare, darin schlummern, als man gewöhnlich annimmt. Tiefe Wut und Schmerz und Zerstörungsucht.

Mendelssohn ist wie ein Mensch, der nur lustig ist, wenn alles ohnehin lustig ist, oder gut, wenn alle um ihn gut sind, und nicht eigentlich wie ein Baum, der fest steht, wie er steht, was immer um ihn vorgehen mag. Ich selber bin auch so ähnlich und neige dazu, es zu sein.

Mein Ideal ist eine gewisse Kühle. Ein Tempel, der den Leidenschaften als Umgebung dient, ohne in sie hineinzureden.

Ich denke oft darüber, ob mein Kulturideal ein neues, d. h. ein zeitgemäßes oder eines aus der Zeit Schumanns ist. Zum mindesten scheint es mir eine Fortsetzung dieses Ideals zu sein, und zwar nicht die Fortsetzung, die es damals tatsächlich erhalten hat. Also unter Ausschluß der zweiten Hälfte des 19. Jahrhunderts. Ich muß sagen, daß das rein instinktmäßig so geworden ist, und nicht als Resultat einer Überlegung.

Each morning you have to break through the dead rubble afresh so as to reach the living warm seed.

A new word is like a fresh seed sewn on the ground of the discussion.

With my full philosophical rucksack I can only climb slowly up the mountain of mathematics.

Mendelssohn is not a peak, but a plateau. His Englishness.

No one can think a thought for me in the way no one can don my hat for me.

Anyone who listens to a child's crying and understands what he hears will know that it harbours dormant psychic forces, terrible forces different from anything commonly assumed. Profound rage, pain and lust for destruction.

Mendelssohn is like a man who is only jolly when the people he is with are all jolly anyway, or like one who is only good when he is surrounded by good men; he does not have the integrity of a tree which stands firmly in its place whatever may be going on around it. I too am like that and am attracted to being so.

My ideal is a certain coolness. A temple providing a setting for the passions without meddling with them.

I often wonder whether my cultural ideal is a new one, i.e. contemporary, or whether it derives from Schumann's time. It does at least strike me as continuing that ideal, though not in the way it was actually continued at the time. That is to say, the second half of the Nineteenth Century has been left out. This, I ought to say, has been a purely instinctive development and not the result of reflection.

Wenn wir an die Zukunft der Welt denken, so meinen wir immer den Ort, wo sie sein wird, wenn sie so weiter läuft, wie wir sie jetzt laufen sehen, und denken nicht, daß sie nicht gerade läuft, sondern in einer Kurve, und ihre Richtung sich konstant ändert.

Ich glaube, das gute Österreichische (Grillparzer, Lenau, Bruckner, Labor) ist besonders schwer zu verstehen. Es ist in gewissem Sinne *subtiler* als alles andere, und seine Wahrheit ist nie auf Seiten der Wahrscheinlichkeit.

Wenn etwas gut ist, so ist es auch göttlich. Damit ist seltsamerweise meine Ethik zusammengefaßt.
Nur das übernatürliche kann das Übernatürliche ausdrücken.

Man kann die Menschen nicht zum Guten führen; man kann sie nur irgendwohin führen. Das Gute liegt außerhalb des Tatsachenraums.

1930

Ich sagte neulich zu Arvid[1], mit dem ich im Kino einen uralten Film gesehen hatte: Ein jetziger Film verhielte sich zum alten, wie ein heutiges Automobil zu einem von vor 25 Jahren. Er wirkt ebenso lächerlich und ungeschickt, wie diese und die Verbesserung des Films entspricht einer technischen Verbesserung, wie der des Automobils. Sie entspricht nicht der Verbesserung – wenn man das so nennen darf – eines Kunststils. Ganz ähnlich müßte es auch in der modernen Tanzmusik gehen. Ein Jazztanz müßte sich verbessern lassen, wie ein Film. Das, was alle diese Entwicklingen von dem Werden eines *Stils* unterscheidet, ist die Unbeteiligung des Geistes.

Ich habe einmal, und vielleicht mit Recht, gesagt: Aus der früheren Kultur wird ein Trümmerhaufen und am Schluß ein Aschenhaufen werden, aber es werden Geister über der Asche schweben.

Der Unterschied zwischen einem guten und einem schlechten Architekten besteht heute darin, daß dieser jeder Versuchung erliegt, während der rechte ihr standhält.

---

[1] Arvid Sjögren, ein Freund und Verwandter von L. W.

When we think of the world's future, we always mean the destination it will reach if it keeps going in the direction we can see it going in now; it does not occur to us that its path is not a straight line but a curve, constantly changing direction.

I think good Austrian work (Grillparzer, Lenau, Bruckner, Labor) is particularly hard to understand. There is a sense in which it is *subtler* than anything else and the truth it expresses never leans towards plausibility.

What is good is also divine. Queer as it sounds, that sums up my ethics. Only something supernatural can express the Supernatural.

You cannot lead people to what is good; you can only lead them to some place or other. The good is outside the space of facts.

1930

I recently said to Arvid,[1] after I had been watching a very old film with him in the cinema: A modern film is to an old one as a present-day motor car is to one built 25 years ago. The impression it makes is just as ridiculous and clumsy and the way film-making has improved is comparable to the sort of technical improvement we see in cars. It is not to be compared with the improvement – if it's right to call it that – of an artistic style. It must be much the same with modern dance music too. A jazz dance, like a film, must be something that can be improved. What distinguishes all these developments from the formation of a *style* is that spirit plays no part in them.

I once said, perhaps rightly: The earlier culture will become a heap of rubble and finally a heap of ashes, but spirits will hover over the ashes.

Today the difference between a good and a poor architect is that the poor architect succumbs to every temptation and the good one resists it.

---

[1] Arvid Sjögren, a friend and relation of L. W.

Die Lücke, die der Organismus des Kunstwerks aufweist, will man mit Stroh ausstopfen, um aber das Gewissen zu beruhigen, nimmt man das *beste* Stroh.

Wenn Einer die Lösung des Problems des Lebens gefunden zu haben glaubt, und sich sagen wollte, jetzt ist alles ganz leicht, so brauchte er sich zu seiner Widerlegung nur erinnern, daß es eine Zeit gegeben hat, wo diese »Lösung« nicht gefunden war; aber auch zu *der* Zeit mußte man leben können, und im Hinblick auf sie erscheint die gefundene Lösung wie ein Zufall. Und so geht es uns in der Logik. Wenn es eine »Lösung« der logischen (philosophischen) Probleme gäbe, so müßten wir uns nur vorhalten, daß sie ja einmal nicht gelöst waren (und auch da mußte man leben und denken können).

Engelmann sagte mir, wenn er zu Hause in seiner Lade voll von seinen Manuskripten krame, so kämen sie ihm so wunderschön vor, daß er denke, sie wären es wert, den anderen Menschen gegeben zu werden. (Das sei auch der Fall, wenn er Briefe seiner verstorbenen Verwandten durchsehe.) Wenn er sich aber eine Auswahl davon herausgegeben denkt, so verliere die Sache jeden Reiz und Wert und werde unmöglich. Ich sagte, wir hatten hier einen Fall ähnlich folgendem: Es könnte nichts merkwürdiger sein, als einen Menschen bei irgend einer ganz einfachen alltäglichen Tätigkeit, wenn er sich unbeobachtet glaubt, zu sehen. Denken wir uns ein Theater, der Vorhang ginge auf und wir sähen einen Menschen allein in seinem Zimmer auf und ab gehen, sich eine Zigarette anzünden, sich niedersetzen, u.s.f., so, daß wir plötzlich von außen einen Menschen sähen, wie man sich sonst nie sehen kann; wenn wir quasi ein Kapitel einer Biographie mit eigenen Augen sähen, – das müßte unheimlich und wunderbar zugleich sein. Wunderbarer als irgend etwas, was ein Dichter auf der Bühne spielen oder sprechen lassen könnte, wir würden das Leben selbst sehen. – Aber das sehen wir ja alle Tage, und es macht uns nicht den mindesten Eindruck! Ja, aber wir sehen es nicht in *der* Perspektive. – So, wenn E. seine Schriften ansieht und sie wunderbar findet (die er doch einzeln nicht veröffentlichen möchte), so sieht er sein Leben als ein Kunstwerk Gottes, und als das ist es allerdings betrachtenswert, jedes Leben und Alles. Doch kann nur der Künstler das Einzelne so darstellen, daß es uns als Kunstwerk erscheint; jene Manuskripte verlieren *mit Recht* ihren Wert, wenn man sie einzeln, und überhaupt, wenn man sie *unvoreingenommen*, das heißt, ohne schon vorher begeistert zu sein, betrachtet. Das Kunstwerk zwingt uns – sozusagen – zu der richtigen Perspektive, ohne die Kunst aber ist der Gegenstand ein Stück Natur, wie jedes andre, und daß *wir* es durch die Begeisterung erheben können, das berechtigt niemand es uns vorzusetzen. (Ich muß immer an eine jener faden Naturaufnahme[n] denken, die der, der sie aufgenommen interessant findet, weil er dort selbst war, etwas erlebt hat; der

A crack is showing in the work of art's organic unity and one tries to stuff it with straw, but to quieten one's conscience one uses only the *best* straw.

If anyone should think he has solved the problem of life and feel like telling himself that everything is quite easy now, he can see that he is wrong just by recalling that there was a time when this "solution" had not been discovered; but it must have been possible to live *then* too and the solution which has now been discovered seems fortuitous in relation to how things were then. And it is the same in the study of logic. If there were a "solution" to the problems of logic (philosophy) we should only need to caution ourselves that there was a time when they had not been solved (and even at that time people must have known how to live and think).

Engelmann told me that when he rummages round at home in a drawer full of his own manuscripts, they strike him as so splendid that he thinks it would be worth making them available to other people. (He says it's the same when he is reading through letters from his dead relations.) But when he imagines publishing a selection of them the whole business loses its charm and value and becomes impossible. I said that was like the following case: Nothing could be more remarkable than seeing a man who thinks he is unobserved performing some quite simple everyday activity. Let us imagine a theatre; the curtain goes up and we see a man alone in a room, walking up and down, lighting a cigarette, sitting down, etc. so that suddenly we are observing a human being from outside in a way that ordinarily we can never observe ourselves; it would be like watching a chapter of biography with our own eyes, – surely this would be uncanny and wonderful at the same time. We should be observing something more wonderful than anything a playwright could arrange to be acted or spoken on the stage: life itself. – But then we do see this every day without its making the slightest impression on us! True enough, but we do not see it from *that* point of view. – Well, when E. looks at what he has written and finds it marvellous (even though he would not care to publish any of the pieces individually), he is seeing his life as a work of art created by God and, as such, it is certainly worth contemplating, as is every life and everything whatever. But only an artist can so represent an individual thing as to make it appear to us like a work of art; it is *right* that those manuscripts should lose their value when looked at singly and especially when regarded *disinterestedly*, i.e. by someone who doesn't feel enthusiastic about them in advance. A work of art forces us – as one might say – to see it in the right perspective but, in the absence of art, the object is just a fragment of nature like any other; *we* may exalt it through our enthusiasm but that does not give anyone else the right to confront us with it. (I keep thinking of one of those insipid snapshots of a piece of scenery which is of interest for the man who

Dritte aber mit berechtigter Kälte betrachtet, wenn es überhaupt gerechtfertigt ist, ein Ding mit Kälte zu betrachten.)

Nun scheint mir aber, gibt es außer der Arbeit des Künstlers noch eine andere, die Welt sub specie aeterni einzufangen. Es ist – glaube ich – der Weg des Gedankens, der gleichsam über die Welt hinfliege und sie so läßt, wie sie ist – sie von oben vom Fluge betrachtend.

Ich lese in Renans ›Peuple d'Israël‹: »La naissance, la maladie, la mort, le délire, la catalepsie, le sommeil, les rêves frappaient infiniment, et, même aujourd'hui, il n'est donné qu'à un petit nombre de voir clairement que ces phénomènes ont leurs causes dans notre organisation.«[1]

Im Gegenteil, es besteht gar kein Grund, sich über diese Dinge zu wundern, weil sie so alltäglich sind. Wenn sich der primitive Mensch über sie wundern *muß*, wieviel mehr der Hund und der Affe. Oder nimmt man an, daß die Menschen quasi plötzlich aufgewacht sind, und diese Dinge, die schon immer da waren, nun plötzlich bemerken und begreiflicherweise erstaunt waren? – Ja, etwas Ähnliches könnte man sogar annehmen; aber nicht, daß sie diese Dinge zum erstenmal wahrnehmen, sondern, daß sie plötzlich anfangen, sich über sie zu wundern. Das aber hat wieder nichts mit ihrer Primitivität zu tun. Es sei denn, daß man es primitiv nennt, sich nicht über die Dinge zu wundern, dann aber sind gerade die heutigen Menschen und Renan selbst primitiv, wenn er glaubt, die Erklärung der Wissenschaft könne das Staunen heben.

Als ob der Blitz heute alltäglicher oder weniger staunenswert wäre als vor 2000 Jahren.

Zum Staunen muß der Mensch – und vielleicht Völker – aufwachen. Die Wissenschaft ist ein Mittel um ihn wieder einzuschläfern.

D. h., es ist einfach falsch zu sagen: Natürlich, diese primitiven Völker *mußten* alle Phänomene anstaunen. Vielleicht aber richtig, diese Völker *haben* alle Dinge ihrer Umgebung angestaunt. – Daß sie sie anstaunen mußten, ist ein primitiver Aberglaube. (Wie der, daß sie sich vor allen Naturkräften fürchten *mußten*, und wir uns natürlich nicht fürchten brauchen. Aber die Erfahrung mag lehren, daß gewisse primitive Stämme sehr zur Furcht vor den Naturphänomenen neigen. – Es ist aber nicht ausgeschlossen, daß *hoch*zivilisierte Völker wieder zu eben dieser Furcht neigen werden, und ihre Zivilisation und die wissenschaftliche Kenntnis kann sie nicht davor schützen. Freilich ist es wahr, daß der *Geist*, in dem die Wissenschaft heute betrieben wird, mit einer solchen Furcht nicht vereinbar ist.)

---

[1] Ernest Renan: *Histoire du Peuple d'Israël*, Tome Premier, Chapitre III.

took it because he was there himself and experienced something; but someone else will quite justifiably look at it coldly, in so far as it is ever justifiable to look at something coldly.)

But it seems to me too that there is a way of capturing the world sub specie aeterni other than through the work of the artist. Thought has such a way – so I believe – it is as though it flies above the world and leaves it as it is – observing it from above, in flight.

In Renan's 'Peuple d'Israël' I read: "Birth, sickness, death, madness, catalepsy, sleep, dreams, all made an immense impression and, even nowadays, only a few have the gift of seeing clearly that these phenomena have causes within our constitution."[1]

On the contrary there is absolutely no reason to wonder at these things, because they are such everyday occurrences. If primitive men can't help but wonder at them, how much more so dogs and monkeys. Or is it being assumed that men, as it were, suddenly woke up and, noticing for the first time these things that had always been there, were understandably amazed? – Well, as a matter of fact we might assume something like this; though not that they become aware of these things for the first time but that they do suddenly start to wonder at them. But this again has nothing to do with their being primitive. Unless it is called primitive not to wonder at things, in which case the people of today are really the primitive ones, and Renan himself too if he supposes that scientific explanation could intensify wonderment.

As though lightning were more commonplace or less astounding today than 2000 years ago.

Man has to awaken to wonder – and so perhaps do peoples. Science is a way of sending him to sleep again.

In other words it's just false to say: Of course, these primitive peoples couldn't help wondering at everything. Though perhaps it is true that these peoples *did* wonder at all the things around them. – To suppose they couldn't help wondering at them is a primitive superstition. (It is like supposing that they *had* to be afraid of all the forces of nature, whereas we of course have no need to be afraid. On the other hand we may learn from experience that certain primitive tribes are very strongly inclined to fear natural phenomena. – But we cannot exclude the possibility that *highly* civilized peoples will become liable to this very same fear once again; neither their civilization nor scientific knowledge can protect them against this. All the same it's true enough that the *spirit* in which science is carried on nowadays is not compatible with fear of this kind.)

[1] Ernest Renan: *History of the People of Israel*, Vol. I, Chapter III.

Wenn Renan vom ›bon sens précoce‹ der semitischen Rassen spricht (eine Idee, die mir vor langer Zeit schon vorgeschwebt ist), so ist das das *Undichterische*, unmittelbar auf's Konkrete gehende. Das, was meine Philosophie bezeichnet.

Die Dinge liegen unmittelbar da vor unsern Augen, kein Schleier über ihnen. – Hier trennen sich Religion und Kunst.

Zu einem Vorwort:[1]

Dieses Buch ist für diejenigen geschrieben, die dem Geist, in dem es geschrieben ist, freundlich gegenüberstehen. Dieser Geist ist, glaube ich, ein anderer als der des großen Stromes der europäischen und amerikanischen Zivilisation. Der Geist dieser Zivilisation, dessen Ausdruck die Industrie, Architektur, Musik, der Faschismus und Sozialismus unserer Zeit ist, ist dem Verfasser fremd und unsympathisch. Dies ist kein Werturteil. Nicht, als ob er glaubte, daß was sich heute als Architektur ausgibt, Architektur wäre, und nicht, als ob er dem, was moderne Musik heißt, nicht das größte Mißtrauen entgegenbrächte (ohne ihre Sprache zu verstehen), aber das Verschwinden der Künste rechtfertigt kein absprechendes Urteil über eine Menschheit. Denn echte und starke Naturen wenden sich eben in dieser Zeit von dem Gebiet der Künste ab, und anderen Dingen zu, und der Wert des Einzelnen kommt irgendwie zum Ausdruck. Freilich nicht wie zur Zeit einer großen Kultur. Die Kultur ist gleichsam eine große Organisation, die jedem, der zu ihr gehört, seinen Platz anweist, an dem er im Geist des Ganzen arbeiten kann, und seine Kraft kann mit großem Recht an seinem Erfolg im Sinne des Ganzen gemessen werden. Zur Zeit der Unkultur aber zersplittern sich die Kräfte und die Kraft des Einzelnen wird durch entgegengesetzte Kräfte und Reibungswiderstände verbraucht, und kommt nicht in der Länge des durchlaufenen Weges zum Ausdruck, sondern vielleicht nur in der Wärme, die er beim Überwinden der Reibungswiderstände erzeugt hat. Aber Energie bleibt Energie, und wenn so das Schauspiel, das dieses Zeitalter bietet, auch nicht das des Werdens eines großen Kulturwerkes ist, in dem die Besten dem gleichen großen Zweck zuarbeiten, sondern das wenig imposante Schauspiel einer Menge, deren Beste nur privaten Zielen nachstreben, so dürfen wir nicht vergessen, daß es auf das Schauspiel nicht ankommt.

Ist es mir so klar, daß das Verschwinden einer Kultur nicht das Verschwinden menschlichen Wertes bedeutet, sondern bloß gewisser Ausdrucksmittel dieses Werts, so bleibt dennoch die Tatsache bestehen, daß ich dem Strom der europäischen Zivilisation ohne Sympathie zusehe, ohne Verständnis für die Ziele, wenn sie welche hat. Ich schreibe also eigentlich für Freunde, welche in Winkeln der Welt verstreut sind.

[1] Eine frühere Fassung des gedruckten Vorworts zu *Philosophische Bemerkungen*. Herausgegeben von Rush Rhees. Basil Blackwell, Oxford 1964.

What Renan calls the 'bon sens précoce' of the semitic races (an idea which had occurred to me too a long time ago) is their *unpoetic* mentality, which heads straight for what is concrete. This is characteristic of my philosophy.

Things are placed right in front of our eyes, not covered by any veil. – This is where religion and art part company.

Sketch for a Foreword[1]

This book is written for those who are in sympathy with the spirit in which it is written. This is not, I believe, the spirit of the main current of European and American civilization. The spirit of this civilization makes itself manifest in the industry, architecture and music of our time, in its fascism and socialism, and it is alien and uncongenial to the author. This is not a value judgement. It is not, it is true, as though he accepted what nowadays passes for architecture as architecture or did not approach what is called modern music with the greatest suspicion (though without understanding its language), but still, the disappearance of the arts does not justify judging disparagingly the human beings who make up this civilization. For in times like these, genuine strong characters simply leave the arts aside and turn to other things and somehow the worth of the individual man finds expression. Not, to be sure, in the way it would at a time of high culture. A culture is like a big organization which assigns each of its members a place where he can work in the spirit of the whole; and it is perfectly fair for his power to be measured by the contribution he succeeds in making to the whole enterprise. In an age without culture on the other hand forces become fragmented and the power of an individual man is used up in overcoming opposing forces and frictional resistances; it does not show in the distance he travels but perhaps only in the heat he generates in overcoming friction. But energy is still energy and even if the spectacle which our age affords us is not the formation of a great cultural work, with the best men contributing to the same great end, so much as the unimpressive spectacle of a crowd whose best members work for purely private ends, still we must not forget that the spectacle is not what matters.

I realize then that the disappearance of a culture does not signify the disappearance of human value, but simply of certain means of expressing this value, yet the fact remains that I have no sympathy for the current of European civilization and do not understand its goals, if it has any. So I am really writing for friends who are scattered throughout the corners of the globe.

[1] An early draft of the printed foreword to *Philosophical Remarks*, edited by Rush Rhees and translated by Raymond Hargreaves and Roger White (Oxford, Basil Blackwell, 1975).

Ob ich von dem typischen westlichen Wissenschaftler verstanden oder geschätzt werde, ist mir gleichgültig, weil er den Geist, in dem ich schreibe, doch nicht versteht. Unsere Zivilisation ist durch das Wort ›Fortschritt‹ charakterisiert. Der Fortschritt ist ihre Form, nicht eine ihrer Eigenschaften, daß sie fortschreitet. Sie ist typisch aufbauend. Ihre Tätigkeit ist es, ein immer komplizierteres Gebilde zu konstruieren. Und auch die Klarheit dient doch nur wieder diesem Zweck und ist nicht Selbstzweck. Mir dagegen ist die Klarheit, die Durchsichtigkeit, Selbstzweck.

Es interessiert mich nicht, ein Gebäude aufzuführen, sondern die Grundlagen der möglichen Gebäude durchsichtig vor mir zu haben.

Mein Ziel ist also ein anderes als das der Wissenschaftler, und meine Denkbewegung von der ihrigen verschieden.

Jeder Satz, den ich schreibe, meint immer schon das Ganze, also immer wieder dasselbe und es sind gleichsam nur Ansichten eines Gegenstandes unter verschiedenen Winkeln betrachtet.

Ich könnte sagen: Wenn der Ort, zu dem ich gelangen will, nur auf einer Leiter zu ersteigen wäre, gäbe ich es auf, dahin zu gelangen. Denn dort, wo ich wirklich hin muß, dort muß ich eigentlich schon sein.

Was auf einer Leiter erreichbar ist, interessiert mich nicht.

Die erste Bewegung reiht einen Gedanken an den anderen, die andere zielt immer wieder nach demselben Ort.

Die eine Bewegung baut und nimmt Stein auf Stein in die Hand, die andere greift immer wieder nach demselben.

Die Gefahr eines langen Vorworts[1] ist die, daß der Geist eines Buchs sich in diesem zeigen muß, und nicht beschrieben werden kann. Denn ist ein Buch nur für wenige geschrieben, so wird sich das eben dadurch zeigen, daß nur wenige es verstehen. Das Buch muß automatisch die Scheidung derer bewirken, die es verstehen, und die es nicht verstehen. Auch das Vorwort ist eben für die geschrieben, die das Buch verstehen.

Es hat keinen Sinn jemandem etwas zu sagen, was er nicht versteht, auch wenn man hinzusetzt, daß er es nicht verstehen kann. (Das geschieht so oft mit einem Menschen, den man liebt.)

Willst Du nicht, daß gewisse Menschen in ein Zimmer gehen, so hänge ein Schloß vor, wozu sie keinen Schlüssel haben. Aber es ist sinnlos, darüber mit ihnen zu reden, außer Du willst doch, daß sie das Zimmer von außen bewundern!

[1] S. die vorangehende Bemerkung.

It is all one to me whether or not the typical western scientist understands or appreciates my work, since he will not in any case understand the spirit in which I write. Our civilization is characterized by the word 'progress'. Progress is its form rather than making progress being one of its features. Typically it constructs. It is occupied with building an ever more complicated structure. And even clarity is sought only as a means to this end, not as an end in itself. For me on the contrary clarity, perspicuity are valuable in themselves.

I am not interested in constructing a building, so much as in having a perspicuous view of the foundations of possible buildings.

So I am not aiming at the same target as the scientists and my way of thinking is different from theirs.

Each of the sentences I write is trying to say the whole thing, i.e. the same thing over and over again; it is as though they were all simply views of one object seen from different angles.

I might say: if the place I want to get to could only be reached by way of a ladder, I would give up trying to get there. For the place I really have to get to is a place I must already be at now.

Anything that I might reach by climbing a ladder does not interest me.

One movement links thoughts with one another in a series, the other keeps aiming at the same spot.

One is constructive and picks up one stone after another, the other keeps taking hold of the same thing.

The danger in a long foreword[1] is that the spirit of a book has to be evident in the book itself and cannot be described. For if a book has been written for just a few readers that will be clear just from the fact that only a few people understand it. The book must automatically separate those who understand it from those who do not. Even the foreword is written just for those who understand the book.

Telling someone something he does not understand is pointless, even if you add that he will not be able to understand it. (That so often happens with someone you love.)

If you have a room which you do not want certain people to get into, put a lock on it for which they do not have the key. But there is no point in talking to them about it, unless of course you want them to admire the room from outside!

[1] See the previous remark.

Anständigerweise, hänge ein Schloß vor die Türe, das nur denen auffällt, die es öffnen können, und den andern nicht.

Aber es ist richtig zu sagen, daß das Buch, meiner Meinung nach, mit der fortschreitenden europäischen und amerikanischen Zivilisation nichts zu tun hat.

Daß diese Zivilisation vielleicht die notwendige Umgebung dieses Geistes ist, aber daß sie verschiedene Ziele haben.

Alles rituelle (quasi Hohepriesterische) ist streng zu vermeiden, weil es unmittelbar in Fäulnis übergeht.

Ein Kuß ist freilich auch ein Ritus und er fault nicht, aber eben nur soviel Ritus ist erlaubt, als so echt ist, wie ein Kuß.

Es ist eine große Versuchung den Geist explicit machen zu wollen.

Wo man an die Grenze seiner eigenen Anständigkeit stößt, dort entsteht quasi ein Wirbel der Gedanken, ein endloser Regreß: Man mag *sagen*, was man will, es führt einen nicht weiter.

Ich lese in Lessing (über die Bibel)[1]: »Setzt hierzu noch die Einkleidung und den Stil ..., durchaus voll Tautologien, aber solchen, die den Scharfsinn üben, indem sie bald etwas anderes zu sagen scheinen, und doch das nämliche sagen, bald das nämliche zu sagen scheinen, und im Grunde etwas anderes bedeuten oder bedeuten können.«

Wenn ich nicht recht weiß, wie ein Buch anfangen, so kommt das daher, daß noch etwas unklar ist. Denn ich möchte mit dem der Philosophie gegebenen, den geschriebenen und gesprochenen Sätzen, quasi den Büchern, anfangen.

Und hier begegnet man der Schwierigkeit des »Alles fließt«. Und mit ihr ist vielleicht überhaupt anzufangen.

Wer seiner Zeit nur voraus ist, den holt sie einmal ein.

1931

Die Musik scheint manchem eine primitive Kunst zu sein, mit ihren wenigen Tönen und Rhythmen. Aber einfach ist nur ihre Oberfläche, während der Körper, der die Deutung dieses manifesten Inhalts ermöglicht, die ganze

---

[1] Lessing: *Die Erziehung des Menschengeschlechts.* § 48–49.

The honourable thing to do is to put a lock on the door which will be noticed only by those who can open it, not by the rest.

But it's proper to say that I think the book has nothing to do with the progressive civilization of Europe and America.

And that while its spirit may be possible only in the surroundings of this civilization, they have different objectives.

Everything ritualistic (everything that, as it were, smacks of the high priest) must be strictly avoided, because it immediately turns rotten.

Of course a kiss is a ritual too and it isn't rotten, but ritual is permissible only to the extent that it is as genuine as a kiss.

It is a great temptation to try to make the spirit explicit.

When you bump against the limits of your own honesty it is as though your thoughts get into a whirlpool, an infinite regress: You can *say* what you like, it takes you no further.

I have been reading Lessing (on the Bible):[1] "Add to this the verbal clothing and the style . . ., absolutely full of tautologies, but of a kind to exercise one's wits by seeming sometimes to say something different while really saying the same thing and at other times seeming to say the same thing while at bottom meaning, or being capable of meaning, something different."

If I am not quite sure how I should start a book, this is because I am still unclear about something. For I should like to start with the original data of philosophy, written and spoken sentences, with books as it were.

And here we come on the difficulty of "all is in flux". Perhaps that is the very point at which to start.

If someone is merely ahead of his time, it will catch him up one day.

1931

Some people think music a primitive art because it has only a few notes and rhythms. But it is only simple on the surface; its substance on the other hand, which makes it possible to interpret this manifest content, has all the infinite

[1] G. E. Lessing: *The Education of the Human Race*, §§ 48–49.

unendliche Komplexität besitzt, die wir in dem Äußeren der anderen Künste angedeutet finden, und die die Musik verschweigt. Sie ist in gewissem Sinne die raffinierteste aller Künste.

Es gibt Probleme, an die ich nie herankomme, die nicht in meiner Linie oder in meiner Welt liegen. Probleme der abendländischen Gedankenwelt, an die Beethoven (und vielleicht teilweise Goethe) herangekommen ist, und mit denen er gerungen hat, die aber kein Philosoph je angegangen hat (vielleicht ist Nietzsche an ihnen vorbeigekommen). Und vielleicht sind sie für die abendländische Philosophie verloren, d. h., es wird niemand da sein, der den Fortgang dieser Kultur als Epos empfindet, also beschreiben kann. Oder richtiger, sie ist eben kein Epos mehr, oder doch nur für den, der sie von außen betrachtet, und vielleicht hat dies Beethoven vorschauend getan (wie Spengler einmal andeutet). Man könnte sagen, die Zivilisation muß ihren Epiker voraushaben. Wie man den eigenen Tod nur voraussehen und vorausschauend beschreiben, nicht als Gleichzeitiger von ihm berichten kann. Man könnte also sagen: Wenn Du das Epos einer ganzen Kultur beschrieben sehen willst, so mußt Du es unter den Werken der größten dieser Kultur, also zu einer Zeit, suchen, in der das Ende dieser Kultur nur hat *voraus*gesehen werden können, denn später ist niemand mehr da es zu beschreiben. Und so ist es also kein Wunder, wenn es nur in der dunklen Sprache der Vorausahnung geschrieben ist und für die Wenigsten verständlich.

Ich aber komme zu diesen Problemen überhaupt nicht. Wenn ich »have done with the world«, so habe ich eine amorphe (durchsichtige) Masse geschaffen, und die Welt mit ihrer ganzen Vielfältigkeit bleibt, wie eine uninteressante Gerümpelkammer, links liegen.
    Oder vielleicht richtiger: das ganze Resultat der ganzen Arbeit ist das Linksliegenlassen der Welt. (Das In-die-Rumpelkammer-werfen der ganzen Welt.)

Eine Tragik gibt es in dieser Welt (der meinen) nicht, und damit all das Unendliche nicht, was eben die Tragik (als Ergebnis) hervorbringt.
    Es ist sozusagen alles in dem Weltäther löslich; es gibt keine Härten.
    Das heißt, die Härte und der Konflikt wird nicht zu etwas Herrlichem, sondern zu einem *Fehler*.

Der Konflikt löst sich etwa, wie die Spannung einer Feder in einem Mechanismus, den man schmilzt (oder in Salpetersäure auflöst). In dieser Lösung gibt es keine Spannungen mehr.

complexity that's suggested in the external forms of other arts and that music conceals. There is a sense in which it is the most sophisticated art of all.

There are problems I never get anywhere near, which do not lie in my path or are not part of my world. Problems of the intellectual world of the West that Beethoven (and perhaps Goethe to a certain extent) tackled and wrestled with, but which no philosopher has ever confronted (perhaps Nietzsche passed by them). And perhaps they are lost as far as western philosophy is concerned, i.e. no one will be there capable of experiencing, and hence describing, the progress of this culture as an epic. Or more precisely, it just no longer is an epic, or is so only for someone looking at it from outside, which is perhaps what Beethoven did with prevision (as Spengler hints somewhere). It might be said that civilization can only have its epic poets in advance. Just as a man cannot report his own death when it happens, but only foresee it and describe it as something lying in the future. So it might be said: If you want to see an epic description of a whole culture, you will have to look at the works of its greatest figures, hence at works composed when the end of this culture could only be *fore*seen, because later on there will be nobody left to describe it. So it's not to be wondered at that it should only be written in the obscure language of prophecy, comprehensible to very few indeed.

But I do not come near these problems. When I "have done with the world" I shall have created an amorphous (transparent) mass and the world in all its variety will be left on one side like an uninteresting lumber room.

Or perhaps more precisely: the whole outcome of this entire work is for the world to be set on one side. (A throwing-into-the-lumber-room of the whole world.)

In this world (mine) there is no tragedy, nor is there that infinite variety of circumstance which gives rise to tragedy (as its result).

It is as though everything were soluble in the aether of the world; there are no hard surfaces.

What that means is that hardness and conflict do not become something splendid, but a *defect*.

Conflict is dissipated in much the same way as is the tension of a spring when you melt the mechanism (or dissolve it in nitric acid). This dissolution eliminates all tensions.

Wenn ich sage, daß mein Buch nur für einen kleinen Kreis von Menschen bestimmt ist (wenn man das einen Kreis nennen kann), so will ich damit nicht sagen, daß dieser Kreis, meiner Auffassung nach, die Elite der Menschheit ist, aber es sind die Menschen, an die ich mich wende (nicht weil sie besser oder schlechter sind als die andern, sondern), weil sie mein Kulturkreis sind, gleichsam die Menschen meines Vaterlandes, im Gegensatz zu den anderen, die mir *fremd* sind.

Die Grenze der Sprache zeigt sich in der Unmöglichkeit, die Tatsache zu beschreiben, die einem Satz entspricht (seine Übersetzung ist), ohne eben den Satz zu wiederholen.
   (Wir haben es hier mit der Kantischen Lösung des Problems der Philosophie zu tun.)

Kann ich sagen, das Drama hat seine eigene Zeit, die nicht ein Abschnitt der historischen Zeit ist? D. h., ich kann in ihm von früher und später reden, aber die Frage hat *keinen Sinn*, ob die Ereignisse etwa vor oder nach Cäsars Tod geschehen sind.

Beiläufig gesprochen, hat es nach der alten Auffassung – etwa der der (großen) westlichen Philosophen – zwei Arten von Problemen im wissenschaftlichen Sinne gegeben: wesentliche, große, universelle, und unwesentliche, quasi accidentelle Probleme. Und dagegen ist unsere Auffassung, daß es kein *großes*, wesentliches Problem im Sinne der Wissenschaft gibt.

Struktur und Gefühl in der Musik. Die Gefühle begleiten das Auffassen eines Musikstücks, wie sie die Vorgänge des Lebens begleiten.

Der Ernst Labors ist ein sehr später Ernst.

Das Talent ist ein Quell, woraus immer wieder neues Wasser fließt. Aber diese Quelle wird wertlos, wenn sie nicht in rechter Weise benutzt wird.

»Was der Gescheite weiß, ist schwer zu wissen.« Hat die Verachtung Goethes für das Experiment im Laboratorium und die Aufforderung in die freie Natur

If I say that my book is meant for only a small circle of people (if it can be called a circle), I do not mean that I believe this circle to be the élite of mankind; but it does comprise those to whom I turn (not because they are better or worse than others but) because they form my cultural milieu, my fellow citizens as it were, in contrast to the rest who are *foreign* to me.

The limit of language is shown by its being impossible to describe the fact which corresponds to (is the translation of) a sentence, without simply repeating the sentence.

(This has to do with the Kantian solution of the problem of philosophy.)

Can I say that a play has a time of its own, which is not a segment of historical time? I.e. I can distinguish earlier and later within it but there is *no sense* to the question whether the events in it take place, say, before or after Caesar's death.

By the way, the old idea – roughly that of the (great) western philosophers – was that there were two kinds of problem in the scientific sense: essential, big, universal problems and inessential, as it were accidental, ones. According to our conception on the other hand we cannot speak in science of a *great*, essential problem.

Structure and feeling in music. Feelings accompany our apprehension of a piece of music in the way they accompany the events of our life.

Labor's is a very late seriousness.

Talent is a spring from which fresh water is constantly flowing. But this spring loses its value if it is not used in the right way.

"What an intelligent man knows is hard to know." Does Goethe's contempt for laboratory experiment and his exhortation to us to go out and learn from

zu gehen und dort zu lernen, hat dies mit dem Gedanken zu tun, daß die Hypothese (unrichtig aufgefaßt) schon eine Fälschung der Wahrheit ist? Und mit dem Anfang, den ich mir jetzt für mein Buch denke, der in einer Naturbeschreibung bestehen könnte?

Wenn Menschen eine Blume oder ein Tier häßlich finden, so stehen sie immer unter dem Eindruck, es seien Kunstprodukte. »Es schaut so aus, wie . . .«, heißt es dann. Das wirft ein Licht auf die Bedeutung der Worte »häßlich« und »schön«.

Die liebliche Temperaturdifferenz der Teile eines menschlichen Körpers.

Es ist beschämend, sich als leerer Schlauch zeigen zu müssen, der nur vom Geist aufgeblasen wird.

Niemand will den Andern gerne verletzt haben; darum tut es jedem so gut, wenn der Andere sich nicht verletzt zeigt. Niemand will gerne eine beleidigte Leberwurst vor sich haben. Das merke Dir. Es ist viel leichter, dem Beleidigten geduldig – und duldend – aus dem Weg gehen, als ihm freundlich entgegengehen. Dazu gehört auch Mut.

Zu dem, der Dich nicht mag, gut zu sein, erfordert nicht nur viel Gutmütigkeit, sondern auch viel *Takt*.

Wir kämpfen mit der Sprache.
Wir stehen im Kampf mit der Sprache.

Die Lösung philosophischer Probleme verglichen mit dem Geschenk im Märchen, das im Zauberschloß zauberisch erscheint und wenn man es draußen beim Tag betrachtet, nichts ist, als ein gewöhnliches Stück Eisen (oder dergleichen).

untrammelled nature have anything to do with the idea that a hypothesis (interpreted in the wrong way) already falsifies the truth? And is it connected with the way I am now thinking of starting my book – with a description of nature?

Flowers or animals that people find ugly always strike them like artefacts. "It looks like a . . .", they say. This illuminates the meaning of the words "ugly" and "beautiful".

The delightful way the various parts of a human body differ in temperature.

It is humiliating to have to appear like an empty tube which is simply inflated by a mind.

No one likes having offended another person; hence everyone feels so much better if the other person doesn't show he's been offended. Nobody likes being confronted by a wounded spaniel. Remember that. It is much easier patiently – and tolerantly[1] – to avoid the person you have injured than to approach him as a friend. You need courage for that.

To treat somebody well when he does not like you, you need to be not only very good natured, but very *tactful* too.

We are struggling with language.
We are engaged in a struggle with language.

The solution of philosophical problems can be compared with a gift in a fairy tale: in the magic castle it appears enchanted and if you look at it outside in daylight it is nothing but an ordinary bit of iron (or something of the sort).

---

[1] In the German there is a play on the words *geduldig* and *duldend*, which intensifies the irony and which I have been unable to catch in English. (Tr.)

Der Denker gleicht sehr dem Zeichner, der alle Zusammenhänge nach-
zeichnen will.

Kompositionen, die am Klavier, auf dem Klavier, komponiert sind, solche, die
mit der Feder denkend und solche, die mit dem inneren Ohr allein
komponiert sind, müssen einen *ganz* verschiedenen Charakter tragen und
einen Eindruck ganz verschiedener Art machen.

Ich glaube bestimmt, daß Bruckner nur mit dem inneren Ohr und einer
Vorstellung vom spielenden Orchester, Brahms mit der Feder, komponiert
hat. Das ist natürlich einfacher dargestellt, als es ist. *Eine* Charakteristik aber ist
damit getroffen.

Eine Tragödie könnte doch immer anfangen mit den Worten: »Es wäre gar
nichts geschehen, wenn nicht . . .«

(Wenn er nicht mit einem Zipfel seines Kleides in die Maschine geraten
wäre?)

Aber ist das nicht eine einseitige Betrachtung der Tragödie, die sie nur
zeigen läßt, daß eine Begegnung unser ganzes Leben entscheiden kann.

Ich glaube, daß es heute ein Theater geben könnte, wo mit Masken gespielt
würde. Die Figuren wären eben stylisierte Menschen-Typen. In den Schriften
Kraus' ist das deutlich zu sehen. Seine Stücke könnten, oder müßten, in
Masken aufgeführt werden. Dies entspricht natürlich einer gewissen
Abstraktheit dieser Produkte. Und das Maskentheater ist, wie ich es meine,
überhaupt der Ausdruck eines spiritualistischen Charakters. Es werden daher
auch vielleicht nur die Juden zu diesem Theater neigen.

Frida Schanz:

Nebeltag. Der graue Herbst geht um.
  Das Lachen scheint verdorben;
  die Welt liegt heut so stumm,
  als sei sie nachts gestorben.
  Im golden roten Hag
  brauen die Nebeldrachen;
  und schlummernd liegt der Tag.
  Der Tag will nicht erwachen.

A thinker is very much like a draughtsman whose aim it is to represent all the interrelations between things.

Pieces of music composed at the piano, on the keyboard, those thought out with pen on paper and those just composed with imagined sounds in the head must all be quite different in character and make quite different kinds of impression.

I am sure Bruckner composed just by imagining the sound of the orchestra in his head, Brahms with pen on paper. Of course this is an over-simplification. But it does highlight *one* feature.

Every tragedy could really start with the words: "Nothing would have happened had it not been that. . . ."

(Had he not got caught in the machine by the tip of his clothing?)

But surely that is a one-sided view of tragedy, to think of it merely as showing that an encounter can decide one's whole life.

I think it would be possible now to have a form of theatre played in masks. The characters would simply be stylized human types. You can see this clearly in Kraus's writings. His pieces could be, or should be, performed in masks. Of course this goes with a certain abstractness, typical of these works. And as I see it, masked theatre is anyway the expression of an intellectualistic character. And for the same reason perhaps it is a theatrical form that will attract only Jews.

Frida Schanz:

Foggy day. Grey autumn haunts us.
      Laughter seems tainted;
      the world is as silent today
      as though it had died last night.
      In the red-gold hedge
      fog monsters are brewing;
      and the day lies asleep.
      The day will not awaken.

Das Gedicht habe ich aus einem »Rösselsprung« entnommen, wo natürlich die Interpunktion fehlte. Ich weiß daher z. B. nicht, ob das Wort »Nebeltag« der Titel ist, oder ob es zur ersten Zeile gehört, wie ich es geschrieben habe. Und es ist merkwürdig, wie trivial das Gedicht klingt, wenn es nicht mit dem Wort »Nebeltag«, sondern mit »Der graue« beginnt. Der Rhythmus des *ganzen* Gedichts ändert sich dadurch.[1]

Was Du geleistet hast, kann Andern nicht mehr bedeuten als Dir selbst.
Soviel als es Dich gekostet hat, soviel werden sie zahlen.

Der Jude ist eine wüste Gegend, unter deren dünner Gesteinschicht aber die feurig-flüssigen Massen des Geistigen liegen.

Grillparzer: »Wie leicht bewegt man sich im Großen und im Fernen, wie schwer faßt sich, was nah und einzeln an. . . .«

Welches Gefühl hätten wir, wenn wir nicht von Christus gehört hätten?
Hätten wir das Gefühl der Dunkelheit und Verlassenheit?
Haben wir es nur insofern nicht als es ein Kind nicht hat, wenn es weiß, daß jemand mit ihm im Zimmer ist?

Religion als Wahnsinn ist Wahnsinn aus Irreligiosität.

Sehe die Photographie von Korsischen Briganten und denke mir: die Gesichter sind zu hart und meines zu weich, als daß das Christentum darauf schreiben könnte. Die Gesichter der Briganten sind schrecklich anzusehen und doch sind sie gewiß nicht weiter von einem guten Leben entfernt und nur auf einer andren Seite desselben selig als ich.

Labor ist, wo er gute Musik schreibt, absolut unromantisch. Das ist ein sehr merkwürdiges und bedeutsames Zeichen.

[1] Var. im Manuskript: »Der *ganze* Rhythmus des Gedichts . . .«

I took this poem from a *"Rösselsprung"*[1] in which of course the punctuation was not shown. So I do not know if the word *"Nebeltag"* ["Foggy day"] is the title, or belongs rather to the first line, as I have written it. And it is queer how trivial the poem sounds if it does not begin with the word *"Nebeltag"*, but with *"Der graue"* ["Grey"]. This changes the rhythm of the *whole* poem.[2]

What you have achieved cannot mean more to others than it does to you.
    Whatever it has cost you, that's what they will pay.

The Jew is a desert region, but underneath its thin layer of rock lies the molten lava of spirit and intellect.

Grillparzer: "It's so easy to wander about amongst great objects in distant regions, so hard to grasp the solitary thing that's right in front of you. . . ."

What would it feel like not to have heard of Christ?
    Should we feel left alone in the dark?
    Do we escape such a feeling simply in the way a child escapes it when he knows there is someone in the room with him?

Religion as madness is a madness springing from irreligiousness.

I look at the photograph of Corsican brigands and reflect: these faces are too hard and mine too soft for Christianity to be able to make a mark on them. The brigands' faces are terrible to look at and yet they are certainly no farther than I am from a good life; it is just that they and I find our salvation on different sides of such a life.

Labor in his good music is completely unromantic. That is a very remarkable and significant characteristic.

[1] This is something like a crossword puzzle. Each space is occupied by a separate syllable. These are joined together to form a meaningful passage by making transpositions according to the rules for the knight's move (=*Rösselsprung*) in chess.
(Tr.)
[2] Variant reading in MS: "the *whole* rhythm of the poem".

Wenn man die sokratischen Dialoge liest, so hat man das Gefühl: welche fürchterliche Zeitvergeudung! Wozu diese Argumente, die nichts beweisen und nichts klären?

Die Geschichte des Peter Schlemihls[1] sollte, wie mir scheint, so lauten: Er verschreibt seine Seele um Geld dem Teufel. Dann reut es ihn und nun verlangt der Teufel den Schatten als Lösegeld. Peter Schlemihl aber bleibt die Wahl seine Seele dem Teufel zu schenken, oder mit dem Schatten auf das Gemeinschaftsleben der Menschen zu verzichten.

Im Christentum sagt der liebe Gott gleichsam zu den Menschen: Spielt nicht Tragödie, das heißt Himmel und Hölle auf Erden. Himmel und Hölle habe *ich* mir vorbehalten.

So könnte Spengler besser verstanden werden, wenn er sagte: ich *vergleiche* verschiedene Kulturperioden dem Leben von Familien; innerhalb der Familie gibt es eine Familienähnlichkiet, während es auch zwischen Mitgliedern verschiedener Familien eine Ähnlichkeit gibt; die Familienähnlichkeit unterscheidet sich von der andern Ähnlichkeit so und so etc. Ich meine: Das Vergleichsobjekt, der Gegenstand, von welchem diese Betrachtungsweise abgezogen ist, muß uns angegeben werden, damit nicht in die Diskussion immer Ungerechtigkeiten einfließen. Denn da wird dann alles, was für das Urbild der Betrachtung stimmt, nolens volens auch von dem Objekt, worauf wir die Betrachtung anwenden behauptet; und behauptet »es *müsse immer* . . .«.
    Das kommt nun daher, daß man den Merkmalen des Urbilds einen Halt in der Betrachtung geben will. Da man aber Urbild und Objekt vermischt, dem Objekt dogmatisch beilegen muß, was nur das Urbild charakterisieren muß. Anderseits glaubt man, die Betrachtung habe nicht die Allgemeinheit, die man ihr geben will, wenn sie nur für den einen Fall wirklich stimmt. Aber das Urbild soll ja eben als solches hingestellt werden; daß es die ganze Betrachtung charakterisiert, ihre Form bestimmt. Es steht also an der Spitze und ist dadurch allgemein gültig, daß es die Form der Betrachtung bestimmt, nicht dadurch, daß alles, was nur von ihm gilt, von allen Objekten der Betrachtung ausgesagt wird.
    Man möchte so bei allen übertriebenen, dogmatisierenden Behauptungen immer fragen: Was ist denn nun daran wirklich wahr? Oder auch: In welchem Fall stimmt denn das nun wirklich?

---

[1] Adelbert von Chamisso, »Peter Schlemihls wundersame Geschichte«.

Reading the Socratic dialogues one has the feeling: what a frightful waste of time! What's the point of these arguments that prove nothing and clarify nothing?

It seems to me that the story of Peter Schlemihl[1] should read like this: He makes his soul over to the Devil for money. Then he repents it and the Devil demands his shadow as a ransom. But Peter Schlemihl still has a choice between giving the Devil his soul and sacrificing, along with his shadow, life in community with other men.

Within Christianity it's as though God says to men: Don't act a tragedy, that's to say, don't enact heaven and hell on earth. Heaven and hell are *my* affair.

Spengler could be better understood if he said: I am *comparing* different cultural epochs with the lives of families; within a family there is a family resemblance, though you will also find a resemblance between members of different families; family resemblance differs from the other sort of resemblance in such and such ways, etc. What I mean is: we have to be told the object of comparison, the object from which this way of viewing things is derived, otherwise the discussion will constantly be affected by distortions. Because willy-nilly we shall ascribe the properties of the prototype to the object we are viewing in its light; and we claim "it *must always* be . . .".

This is because we want to give the prototype's characteristics a purchase on our way of representing things. But since we confuse prototype and object we find ourselves dogmatically conferring on the object properties which only the prototype necessarily possesses. On the other hand we think our view will not have the generality we want it to have if it is really true only of the one case. But the prototype ought to be clearly presented for what it is; so that it characterizes the whole discussion and determines its form. This makes it the focal point, so that its general validity will depend on the fact that it determines the form of discussion rather than on the claim that everything which is true only of it holds too for all the things that are being discussed.

Similarly the question always to ask when exaggerated, dogmatic assertions are made is: What is actually true in this? Or again: In what case is that actually true?

[1] Adelbert von Chamisso, "The Strange Tale of Peter Schlemihl".

Aus dem Simplicissimus: Rätsel der Technik. (Bild: Zwei Professoren vor einer im Bau befindlichen Brücke.) Stimme von oben: »Laß abi – hüah – laß abi sag' i – nacha drah'n mer'n anders um!« – – »Es ist doch unfaßlich, Herr Kollega, daß eine so komplizierte und exakte Arbeit in dieser Sprache zustande kommen kann.«

Man hört immer wieder die Bemerkung, daß die Philosophie eigentlich keinen Fortschritt mache, daß die gleichen philosophischen Probleme, die schon die Griechen beschäftigten, uns noch beschäftigen. Die das aber sagen, verstehen nicht den Grund, warum es so sein muß. Der ist aber, daß unsere Sprache sich gleich geblieben ist und uns immer wieder zu denselben Fragen verführt. Solange es ein Verbum ›sein‹ geben wird, das zu funktionieren scheint wie ›essen‹ und ›trinken‹, solange es Adjektive ›identisch‹, ›wahr‹, ›falsch‹, ›möglich‹ geben wird, solange von einem Fluß der Zeit und von einer Ausdehnung des Raumes die Rede sein wird, usw., usw., solange werden die Menschen immer wieder an die gleichen rätselhaften Schwierigkeiten stoßen, und auf etwas starren, was keine Erklärung scheint wegheben zu können.
    Und dies befriedigt im Übrigen ein Verlangen nach dem Transcendenten, denn, indem sie die »Grenze des menschlichen Verstandes« zu sehen glauben, glauben sie natürlich, über ihn hinaus sehen zu können.

Ich lese: ». . . philosophers are no nearer to the meaning of 'Reality' than Plato got, . . .«. Welche seltsame Sachlage. Wie sonderbar, daß Platon dann überhaupt so weit kommen konnte! Oder, daß wir dann nicht weiter kommen konnten! War es, weil Platon *so* gescheit war?

Kleist schrieb einmal,[1] es wäre dem Dichter am liebsten, er könnte die Gedanken selbst ohne Worte übertragen. (Welch seltsames Eingeständnis.)

Es wird oft gesagt, daß die neue Religion die Götter der alten zu Teufeln stempelt. Aber in Wirklichkeit sind diese dann wohl schon zu Teufeln geworden.

Die Werke der großen Meister sind Sonnen, die um uns her auf- und untergehen. So wird die Zeit für jedes große Werk wiederkommen, das jetzt untergegangen ist.

---

[1] Brief eines Dichters an einen anderen«, 5. Januar 1811.

From *Simplicissimus*: Riddles of technology. (A picture of two professors in front of a bridge under construction.) Voice from above: "Fotch it dahn – coom on fotch it dahn A tell tha – we'll turn it t'other rooad sooin."[1] – "It really is quite incomprehensible, my dear colleague, how anyone can carry out such complicated and precise work in such language."

People say again and again that philosophy doesn't really progress, that we are still occupied with the same philosophical problems as were the Greeks. But the people who say this don't understand why it has to be so. It is because our language has remained the same and keeps seducing us into asking the same questions. As long as there continues to be a verb 'to be' that looks as if it functions in the same way as 'to eat' and 'to drink', as long as we still have the adjectives 'identical', 'true', 'false', 'possible', as long as we continue to talk of a river of time, of an expanse of space, etc. etc., people will keep stumbling over the same puzzling difficulties and find themselves staring at something which no explanation seems capable of clearing up.

And what's more, this satisfies a longing for the transcendent, because in so far as people think they can see the "limits of human understanding", they believe of course that they can see beyond these.

I read: ". . . philosophers are no nearer to the meaning of 'Reality' than Plato got, . . .". What a strange situation. How extraordinary that Plato could have got even as far as he did! Or that we could not get any further! Was it because Plato was so *extremely* clever?

Kleist wrote somewhere[2] that what the poet would most of all like to be able to do would be to convey thoughts by themselves without words. (What a strange admission.)

It is often said that a new religion brands the gods of the old one as devils. But in reality they have probably already become devils by that time.

The works of great masters are suns which rise and set around us. The time will come for every great work that is now in the descendent to rise again.

[1] I am grateful for this rendering to Mr. S. Ellis of the Institute of Dialect and Folk Life Studies at the University of Leeds. (Tr.)
[2] Heinrich von Kleist: "Letter from One Poet to Another", 5th January, 1811.

Mendelssohns Musik, wo sie vollkommen ist, sind musikalische Arabesken. Daher empfinden wir bei ihm jeden Mangel an Strenge peinlich.

Der Jude wird in der westlichen Zivilisation immer mit Maßen gemessen, die auf ihn nicht passen. Daß die griechischen Denker weder im westlichen Sinn Philosophen, noch im westlichen Sinn Wissenschaftler waren, daß die Teilnehmer der Olympischen Spiele nicht Sportler waren und in kein westliches Fach passen, ist vielen klar. Aber so geht es auch den Juden. Und indem uns die Wörter unserer ⟨Sprache⟩[1] als die Maße schlechthin erscheinen, tun wir ihnen immer Unrecht. Und sie werden bald überschätzt, bald unterschätzt. Richtig reiht dabei Spengler Weininger nicht unter die westlichen Philosophen [Denker].

Nichts, was man tut, läßt sich endgültig verteidigen. Sondern nur in Bezug auf etwas anderes Festgesetztes. D. h., es läßt sich kein Grund angeben, warum man *so* handeln soll (oder hat handeln sollen), als der sagt, daß dadurch dieser Sachverhalt hervorgerufen werde, den man wieder als Ziel *hinnehmen* muß.

Das Unaussprechbare (das, was mir geheimnisvoll erscheint und ich nicht auszusprechen vermag) gibt vielleicht den Hintergrund, auf dem das, was ich aussprechen konnte, Bedeutung bekommt.

Die Arbeit an der Philosophie ist – wie vielfach die Arbeit in der Architektur – eigentlich mehr die Arbeit an Einem selbst. An der eignen Auffassung. Daran, wie man die Dinge sieht. (Und was man von ihnen verlangt.)

Der Philosoph kommt leicht in die Lage eines ungeschickten Direktors, der, statt *seine* Arbeit zu tun und nur darauf zu schauen, daß seine Angestellten ihre Arbeit richtig machen, ihnen ihre Arbeit abnimmt und sich so eines Tages mit fremder Arbeit überladen sieht, während die Angestellten zuschauen und ihn kritisieren.

Der Gedanke ist schon vermüdelt und läßt sich nicht mehr gebrauchen. (Eine ähnliche Bemerkung hörte ich einmal von Labor, musikalische Gedanken betreffend.) Wie Silberpapier, das einmal verknittert ist, sich nie mehr ganz glätten läßt. Fast alle meine Gedanken sind etwas verknittert.

[1] Vermutung des Herausgebers.

When it is at its best Mendelssohn's music consists of musical arabesques. That is why we are disconcerted when his work is lacking in rigour.

In western civilization the Jew is always measured on scales which do not fit him. Many people can see clearly enough that the Greek thinkers were neither philosophers in the western sense nor scientists in the western sense, that the participants in the Olympian Games were not sportsmen and do not fit in to any western occupation. But it is the same with the Jews. And by taking the words of our 〈language〉[1] as the only possible standards we constantly fail to do them justice. So at one time they are overestimated, at another underestimated. Spengler is right in this connection not to classify Weininger with the philosophers [thinkers] of the West.

Nothing we do can be defended absolutely and finally. But only by reference to something else that is not questioned. I.e. no reason can be given why you should act (or should have acted) *like this*, except that by doing so you bring about such and such a situation, which again has to be an aim you *accept*.

Perhaps what is inexpressible (what I find mysterious and am not able to express) is the background against which whatever I could express has its meaning.

Working in philosophy – like work in architecture in many respects – is really more a working on oneself. On one's own interpretation. On one's way of seeing things. (And what one expects of them.)

A philosopher easily gets into the position of an incompetent manager who, instead of getting on with his *own* work and just keeping an eye on his employees to make sure they do theirs properly, takes over their work until one day he finds himself overloaded with other people's work, while his employees look on and criticize him.

The idea is worn out by now and no longer usable. (I once heard Labor make a similar remark about musical ideas.) Like silver paper, which can never quite be smoothed out again once it has been crumpled. Nearly all my ideas are a bit crumpled.

[1] Editor's conjecture.

Ich denke tatsächlich mit der Feder, denn mein Kopf weiß oft nichts von dem, was meine Hand schreibt.

Die Philosophen sind oft wie kleine Kinder, die zuerst mit ihrem Bleistift beliebige Striche auf ein Papier kritzeln und dann den Erwachsenen fragen »was ist das?« – Das ging so zu: Der Erwachsene hatte dem Kind öfters etwas vorgezeichnet und gesagt: »das ist ein Mann«, »das ist ein Haus«, usw. Und nun macht das Kind auch Striche und fragt: was ist nun *das*?

Ramsey war ein bürgerlicher Denker. D. h., seine Gedanken hatten den Zweck, die Dinge in einer gegebenen Gemeinde zu ordnen. Er dachte nicht über das Wesen des Staates nach – oder doch nicht gerne – sondern darüber, wie man *diesen* Staat vernünftig einrichten könne. Der Gedanke, daß dieser Staat nicht der einzig mögliche sei, beunruhigte ihn teils, teils langweilte er ihn. Er wollte so geschwind als möglich dahin kommen, über die Grundlagen – *dieses* Staates – nachzudenken. Hier lag seine Fähigkeit und sein eigentliches Interesse; während die eigentlich philosophische Überlegung ihn beunruhigte, bis er ihr Resultat (wenn sie eins hatte) als trivial zur Seite schob.

Es könnte sich eine seltsame Analogie daraus ergeben, daß das Okular auch des riesigsten Fernrohrs nicht größer sein darf,[1] als unser Auge.

Tolstoi: die Bedeutung (Bedeutsamkeit) eines Gegenstandes liegt in seiner allgemeinen Verständlichkeit. – Das ist wahr und falsch. Das, was den Gegenstand schwer verständlich macht, ist – wenn er bedeutend, wichtig, ist – nicht, daß irgendeine besondere Instruktion über abstruse Dinge zu seinem Verständnis erforderlich wäre, sondern der Gegensatz zwischen dem Verstehen des Gegenstandes und dem, was die meisten Menschen sehen *wollen*. Dadurch kann gerade das Naheliegendste am allerschwersten verständlich werden. Nicht eine Schwierigkeit des Verstandes, sondern des Willens, ist zu überwinden.

Wer heute Philosophie lehrt, gibt dem Andern Speise, nicht, weil sie ihm schmecken, sondern um seinen Geschmack zu ändern.

---

[1] Var. im Manuskript: »nicht größer ist«.

I really do think with my pen, because my head often knows nothing about what my hand is writing.

Philosophers often behave like little children who scribble some marks on a piece of paper at random and then ask the grown-up "What's that?" – It happened like this: the grown-up had drawn pictures for the child several times and said: "this is a man", "this is a house", etc. And then the child makes some marks too and asks: what's *this* then?

Ramsey was a bourgeois thinker. I.e. he thought with the aim of clearing up the affairs of some particular community. He did not reflect on the essence of the state – or at least he did not like doing so – but on how *this* state might reasonably be organized. The idea that this state might not be the only possible one in part disquieted him and in part bored him. He wanted to get down as quickly as possible to reflecting on the foundations – of *this* state. This was what he was good at and what really interested him; whereas real philosophical reflection disturbed him until he put its result (if it had one) to one side and declared it trivial.

A curious analogy could be based on the fact that even the hugest telescope has to have[1] an eye-piece no larger than the human eye.

Tolstoy: a thing's significance (importance) lies in its being something everyone can understand. – That is both true and false. What makes a subject hard to understand – if it's something significant and important – is not that before you can understand it you need to be specially trained in abstruse matters, but the contrast between understanding the subject and what most people *want* to see. Because of this the very things which are most obvious may become the hardest of all to understand. What has to be overcome is a difficulty having to do with the will, rather than with the intellect.

A present-day teacher of philosophy doesn't select food for his pupil with the aim of flattering his taste, but with the aim of changing it.

[1] Variant reading in MS for "has to have": "has".

Ich soll nur der Spiegel sein, in welchem mein Leser sein eigenes Denken mit allen seinen Unförmigkeiten sieht, und mit dieser Hilfe zurecht richten kann.

Die Sprache hat für Alle die gleichen Fallen bereit; das ungeheure Netz gut gangbarer Irrwege. Und so sehen wir also Einen nach dem Andern die gleichen Wege gehn, und wissen schon, wo er jetzt abbiegen wird, wo er geradeaus fortgehen wird, ohne die Abzweigung zu bemerken, etc. etc. Ich sollte also an allen Stellen, wo falsche Wege abzweigen, Tafeln aufstellen, die über die gefährlichen Punkte hinweghelfen.

Was Eddington über ›die Richtung der Zeit‹ und den Entropiesatz sagt, läuft darauf hinaus, daß die Zeit ihre Richtung umkehren würde, wenn die Menschen eines Tages anfingen, rückwärts zu gehen. Wenn man will, kann man das freilich so nennen; man muß dann nur darüber klar sein, daß man damit nichts anders sagt als, daß die Menschen ihre Gehrichtung geändert haben.

Einer teilt die Menschen ein, in Käufer und Verkäufer, und vergißt, daß Käufer auch Verkäufer sind. Wenn ich ihn daran erinnere, wird seine Grammatik geändert??

Das eigentliche Verdienst eines Kopernikus oder Darwin war nicht die Entdeckung einer wahren Theorie, sondern eines fruchtbaren neuen Aspekts.

Ich glaube, was Goethe eigentlich hat finden wollen, war keine physiologische, sondern eine psychologische Theorie der Farben.

Eine Beichte muß ein Teil des neuen Lebens sein.

Ich drücke, was ich ausdrücken will, doch immer nur »mit halbem Gelingen« aus. Ja, auch das nicht, sondern vielleicht nur mit einem Zehntel. Das will doch etwas besagen. Mein Schreiben ist oft nur ein »Stammeln«.

Das jüdische »Genie« ist nur ein Heiliger. Der größte jüdische Denker ist nur ein Talent. (Ich z. B.)
    Es ist, glaube ich, eine Wahrheit darin, wenn ich denke, daß ich eigentlich

I ought to be no more than a mirror, in which my reader can see his own thinking with all its deformities so that, helped in this way, he can put it right.

Language sets everyone the same traps; it is an immense network of easily accessible wrong turnings. And so we watch one man after another walking down the same paths and we know in advance where he will branch off, where walk straight on without noticing the side turning, etc. etc. What I have to do then is erect signposts at all the junctions where there are wrong turnings so as to help people past the danger points.

What Eddington says about 'the direction of time' and the law of entropy comes to this: time would change its direction if men should start walking backwards one day. Of course you can call it that if you like; but then you should be clear in your mind that you have said no more than that people have changed the direction they walk in.

Someone divides mankind into buyers and sellers and forgets that buyers are sellers too. If I remind him of this is his grammar changed??

What a Copernicus or a Darwin really achieved was not the discovery of a true theory but of a fertile new point of view.

What Goethe was really seeking, I believe, was not a physiological, but a psychological theory of colours.

A confession has to be a part of your new life.

I never more than half succeed in expressing what I want to express. Actually not as much as that, but by no more than a tenth. That is still worth something. Often my writing is nothing but "stuttering".

Amongst Jews "genius" is found only in the holy man. Even the greatest of Jewish thinkers is no more than talented. (Myself for instance.)
    I think there is some truth in my idea that I really only think reproductively.

in meinem Denken nur reproduktiv bin. Ich glaube, ich habe nie eine Gedankenbewegung *erfunden*, sondern sie wurde mir immer von jemand anderem gegeben. Ich habe sie nur sogleich leidenschaftlich zu meinem Klärungswerk aufgegriffen. So haben mich Boltzmann, Hertz, Schopenhauer, Frege, Russell, Kraus, Loos, Weininger, Spengler, Sraffa beeinflußt. Kann man als ein Beispiel jüdischer Reproduktivität Breuer und Freud heranziehen? – Was ich erfinde, sind neue *Gleichnisse*.

Als ich seinerzeit den Kopf für Drobil modellierte, so war auch die Anregung wesentlich ein Werk Drobils und meine Arbeit war eigentlich wieder die des Klärens. Ich glaube, das Wesentliche ist, daß die Tätigkeit des Klärens mit MUT betrieben werden muß: fehlt der, so wird sie ein bloßes gescheites Spiel.

Der Jude muß im eigentlichen Sinn »sein Sach' auf nichts stellen«. Aber das fällt gerade ihm besonders schwer, weil er, sozusagen, nichts hat. Es ist viel schwerer freiwillig arm zu sein, wenn man arm sein *muß*, als, wenn man auch reich sein könnte.

Man könnte sagen (ob es nun stimmt oder nicht), daß der jüdische Geist nicht im Stande ist, auch nur ein Gräschen oder Blümchen hervorzubringen, daß es aber seine Art ist, das Gräschen oder die Blume, die im andern Geist gewachsen ist, abzuzeichnen und damit ein umfassendes Bild zu entwerfen. Das ist nun nicht die Angabe eines Lasters und es ist alles in Ordnung, solange das nur völlig klar bleibt. Gefährlich wird es erst, wenn man die Art des Jüdischen mit der des Nicht-Jüdischen Werks verwechselt, und besonders, wenn das der Schöpfer des ersteren selbst tut, was so nahe liegt. (Sieht er nicht so stolz aus, als ob er selber gemolken wäre.[1])

Es ist dem jüdischen Geiste typisch, das Werk eines Anderen besser zu verstehen, als der es selbst versteht.

Ich habe mich oft dabei ertappt, wenn ich ein Bild entweder richtig hätte rahmen lassen oder in die richtige Umgebung gehangen hatte, so stolz zu sein, als hätte ich das Bild gemalt. Das ist eigentlich nicht richtig: nicht »so stolz, als hätte ich es gemalt«, sondern so stolz, als hätte ich es malen geholfen, als hätte ich sozusagen einen kleinen Teil davon gemalt. Es ist so, als würde der außerordentliche Arrangeur von Gräsern am Schluß denken, daß er doch, wenigstens ein ganz winziges Gräschen, selbst erzeugt habe. Während er sich

---

[1] Der Satz zwischen Parenthesen stammt aus Wilhelm Buschs Prosadichtung »Eduards Traum«. Der Herausgeber ist Herrn Robert Löffler für diese Auskunft zum Dank verpflichtet.

I don't believe I have ever *invented* a line of thinking, I have always taken one over from someone else. I have simply straightaway seized on it with enthusiasm for my work of clarification. That is how Boltzmann, Hertz, Schopenhauer, Frege, Russell, Kraus, Loos, Weininger, Spengler, Sraffa have influenced me. Can one take the case of Breuer and Freud as an example of Jewish reproductiveness? – What I invent are new *similes*.

At the time I modelled the head for Drobil too the stimulus was essentially a work of Drobil's and my contribution once again was really clarification. What I do think essential is carrying out the work of clarification with COURAGE: otherwise it becomes just a clever game.

The Jew must see to it that, in a literal sense, "all things are as nothing to him".[1] But this is particularly hard for him, since in a sense he has nothing that is peculiarly his. It is much harder to accept poverty willingly when you *have* to be poor than when you might also be rich.

It might be said (rightly or wrongly) that the Jewish mind does not have the power to produce even the tiniest flower or blade of grass; its way is rather to make a drawing of the flower or blade of grass that has grown in the soil of another's mind and to put it into a comprehensive picture. We aren't pointing to a fault when we say this and everything is all right as long as what is being done is quite clear. It is only when the nature of a Jewish work is confused with that of a non-Jewish work that there is any danger, especially when the author of the Jewish work falls into the confusion himself, as he so easily may. (Doesn't he look as proud as though he had produced the milk himself?)[2]

It is typical for a Jewish mind to understand someone else's work better than he understands it himself.

Often, when I have had a picture well framed or have hung it in the right surroundings, I have caught myself feeling as proud as if I had painted the picture myself. That is not quite right: not "as proud as if I had painted it", but as proud as if I had helped to paint it, as if I had, so to speak, painted a little bit of it. It is as though an exceptionally gifted arranger of grasses should eventually come to think that he had produced at least a tiny blade of grass himself. Whereas it ought to be clear to him that his work lies in a different

[1] The line in quotation marks is adapted from the first line of Goethe's poem, "Vanitas! Vanitatum vanitas", which in its turn is the title of the first chapter of Max Stirner's *Der Einzige und sein Eigentum*. Wittgenstein is probably alluding more directly here to Stirner than to Goethe, the sense of whose poem hardly fits the present context. I am indebted to Rush Rhees for drawing my attention to these allusions. (Tr.)
[2] The sentence in brackets is from Wilhelm Busch's prose poem "Edward's Dream". The editor is indebted to Mr. Robert Löffler for this information.

klar sein muß, daß seine Arbeit auf einem gänzlich andern Gebiet liegt. Der
Vorgang der Entstehung auch des winzigsten und schäbigsten Gräschens ist
ihm gänzlich fremd und unbekannt.

Das genaueste Bild eines ganzen Apfelbaumes hat in gewissem Sinne
unendlich viel weniger Ähnlichkeit mit ihm, als das kleinste Maßliebchen mit
dem Baum hat. Und in diesem Sinne ist eine Brucknersche Symphonie mit
einer Symphonie der heroischen Zeit unendlich näher verwandt, als eine
Mahlerische. Wenn diese ein Kunstwerk ist, dann eines *gänzlich* andrer Art.
(Diese Betrachtung aber selbst ist eigentlich Spenglerisch.)

Als ich übrigens in Norwegen war, im Jahre 1913–14, hatte ich eigene
Gedanken, so scheint es mir jetzt wenigstens. Ich meine, es kommt mir so vor,
als hätte ich damals in mir neue Denkbewegungen geboren (aber vielleicht
irre ich mich). Während ich jetzt nur mehr alte anzuwenden scheine.

Rousseau hat etwas Jüdisches in seiner Natur.

Wenn manchmal gesagt wird, die Philosophie eines Menschen sei Temperamentssache, so ist auch darin eine Wahrheit. Die Bevorzugung gewisser
Gleichnisse ist das, was könnte man Temperamentssache nennen und auf ihr
beruht ein viel größerer Teil der Gegensätze, als es scheinen möchte.

»Betrachte diese Beule als ein regelrechtes Glied deines Körpers!« Kann man
das, auf Befehl? Ist es in meiner Macht, willkürlich ein Ideal von meinem
Körper zu haben oder nicht?
    Die Geschichte der Juden wird darum in der Geschichte der europäischen
Völker nicht mit der Ausführlichkeit behandelt, wie es ihr Eingriff in die
europäischen Ereignisse eigentlich verdiente, weil sie als eine Art Krankheit,
und Anomalie, in dieser Geschichte empfunden werden und niemand gern
eine Krankheit mit dem normalen Leben gleichsam auf eine Stufe stellt [und
niemand gern von einer Krankheit als etwas Gleichberechtigtem mit den
gesunden Vorgängen (auch schmerzhafte) im Körper spricht.]
    Man kann sagen: diese Beule kann nur dann als ein Glied des Körpers
betrachtet werden, wenn sich das ganze Gefühl für den Körper ändert (wenn
sich das ganze Nationalgefühl für den Körper ändert). Sonst kann man sie
höchstens *dulden*.
    Vom einzelnen Menschen kann man so eine Duldung erwarten, oder auch,

region altogether. The process through which even the tiniest and meanest blade of grass comes into being is something he has nothing to do with and knows nothing about.

A picture of a complete apple tree, however accurate, is in a certain sense much less like the tree itself than is a little daisy. And in the same sense a symphony by Bruckner is infinitely closer to a symphony from the heroic period than is one by Mahler. If the latter is a work of art it is one of a *totally* different sort. (But this is actually itself a Spenglerian observation.)

Incidentally, when I was in Norway during the year 1913–14 I had some thoughts of my own, or so at least it seems to me now. I mean I have the impression that at that time I brought to life new movements in thinking (but perhaps I am mistaken). Whereas now I seem just to apply old ones.

Rousseau's character has something Jewish about it.

It is sometimes said that a man's philosophy is a matter of temperament, and there is something in this. A preference for certain similes could be called a matter of temperament and it underlies far more disagreements than you might think.

"Look on this tumour as a perfectly normal part of your body!" Can one do that, to order? Do I have the power to decide at will to have, or not to have, an ideal conception of my body?
   Within the history of the peoples of Europe the history of the Jews is not treated as circumstantially as their intervention in European affairs would actually merit, because within this history they are experienced as a sort of disease, and anomaly, and no one wants to put a disease on the same level as normal life [and no one wants to speak of a disease as if it had the same rights as healthy bodily processes (even painful ones)].
   We may say: people can only regard this tumour as a natural part of the body if their whole feeling for the body changes (if the whole national feeling for the body changes). Otherwise the best they can do is *put up with* it.
   You can expect an individual man to display this sort of tolerance, or else to disregard such things; but you cannot expect this of a nation, because it is precisely not disregarding such things that makes it a nation. I.e. there is a

daß er sich über diese Dinge hinwegsetzt; nicht aber von der Nation, die ja
nur dadurch Nation ist, daß sie sich darüber nicht hinwegsctzt. D. h., es ist ein
Widerspruch zu erwarten, daß Einer das alte aesthetische Gefühl für seinen
Körper behalten *und* die Beule willkommen heißen wird.

   Macht und Besitz sind nicht *dasselbe*. Obwohl uns der Besitz auch Macht
gibt. Wenn man sagt, die Juden hätten keinen Sinn für den Besitz, so ist das
wohl vereinbar damit, daß sie gerne reich sind, denn das Geld ist für sie eine
bestimmte Art von Macht, nicht Besitz. (Ich möchte z. B. nicht, daß meine
Leute arm werden, denn ich wünsche ihnen eine gewisse Macht. Freilich
auch, daß sie diese Macht recht gebrauchen möchten.)

Zwischen Brahms und Mendelssohn herrscht entschieden eine gewisse
Verwandtschaft; und zwar meine ich nicht die, welche sich in einzelnen
Stellen in Brahmschen Werken zeigt, die an Mendelssohnsche Stellen
erinnern, sondern man könnte die Verwandtschaft, von der ich rede, dadurch
ausdrücken, daß man sagt, Brahms tue das mit ganzer Strenge, was
Mendelssohn mit halber getan hat. Oder: Brahms ist oft fehlerfreier
Mendelssohn.

Das wäre das Ende eines Themas, das ich nicht weiß. Es fiel mir heute ein, als
ich über meine Arbeit in der Philosophie nachdachte und mir vorsagte: »I
destroy, I destroy, I destroy —«.

* Die Bestimmung der Taktart fehlt im MS. Der Herausgeber ist Herrn Fabian
Dahlström für sachkundige Hilfe bei der Deutung der schwer leslichen Notenschrift
zum großen Dank verpflichtet.

contradiction in expecting someone *both* to retain his former aesthetic feeling for the body and *also* to make the tumour welcome.

Power and possession aren't the *same* thing. Even though possessions also bring us power. If Jews are said not to have any sense of property, that may be compatible with their liking to be rich since for them money is a particular sort of power, not property. (For instance I should not like my people to become poor, since I wish them to have a certain amount of power. Naturally I wish them to use this power properly too.)

There is definitely a certain sort of kinship between Brahms and Mendelssohn; but I do not mean that shown by the individual passages in Brahms's works which are reminiscent of passages by Mendelssohn, – the kinship I am speaking of could be better expressed by saying that Brahms does with complete rigour what Mendelssohn did only half-rigorously. Or: often Brahms is Mendelssohn without the flaws.

That must be the end of a theme which I cannot place. It came into my head today as I was thinking about my philosophical work and saying to myself: "I destroy, I destroy, I destroy —".

* The time signature is not in the MS. The editor is very grateful to Mr. Fabian Dahlström for professional help in interpreting the written music, which was very hard to read.

Man hat manchmal gesagt, daß die Heimlichkeit und Versteckheit der Juden durch die lange Verfolgung hervorgebracht worden sei. Das ist gewiß unwahr; dagegen ist es gewiß, daß sie, trotz dieser Verfolgung, nur darum noch existieren, weil sie die Neigung zu dieser Heimlichkeit haben. Wie man sagen könnte, daß das und das Tier nur darum noch nicht ausgerottet sei, weil es die Möglichkeit oder Fähigkeit hat, sich zu verstekken. Ich meine natürlich nicht, daß man darum diese Möglichkeit preisen soll, durchaus nicht.

Die Musik Bruckners hat nichts mehr von dem langen und schmalen (nordischen?) Gesicht Nestroys, Grillparzers, Haydns etc., sondern hat ganz und gar ein rundes, volles (alpenländisches?) Gesicht, von noch ungemischterem Typus als das Schuberts war.

Die alles gleich machende Gewalt der Sprache, die sich am krassesten im *Wörterbuch* zeigt, und die es möglich macht, daß *die Zeit* personifiziert werden konnte, was nicht weniger merkwürdig ist, als es wäre, wenn wir Gottheiten der logischen Konstanten hätten.

Ein schönes Kleid, das sich in Würmer und Schlangen verwandelt (gleichsam koaguliert), wenn der, welcher es trägt, sich darin selbstgefällig in den Spiegel schaut.

Die Freude an meinen Gedanken ist die Freude an meinem eigenen seltsamen Leben. Ist das Lebensfreude?

1932

Die Philosophen, welche sagen: »nach dem Tod wird ein zeitloser Zustand eintreten«, oder: »mit dem Tod tritt ein zeitloser Zustand ein«, und nicht merken, daß sie im zeitlichen Sinne »nach« und »mit« und »tritt ein« gesagt haben, und, daß die Zeitlichkeit in ihrer Grammatik liegt.

Circa 1932–1934

Erinnere Dich an den Eindruck guter Architektur, daß sie einen Gedanken ausdrückt. Man möchte auch ihr mit einer Geste folgen.

It has sometimes been said that the Jews' secretive and cunning nature is a result of their long persecution. That is certainly untrue; on the other hand it is certain that they continue to exist despite this persecution only because they have an inclination towards such secretiveness. As we may say that this or that animal has escaped extinction only because of its capacity or ability to conceal itself. Of course I do not mean that as a reason for commending such a capacity, not by any means.

In Bruckner's music nothing is left of the long, slender (nordic?) face of Nestroy, Grillparzer, Haydn, etc.; instead its face is completely round and full (alpine?), even purer than Schubert's.

The power language has to make everything look the same, which is most glaringly evident in the *dictionary* and which makes the personification of *time* possible: something no less remarkable than would have been making divinities of the logical constants.

A beautiful garment that is transformed (coagulates, as it were) into worms and serpents if its wearer looks smugly at himself in the mirror.

The delight I take in my thoughts is delight in my own strange life. Is this joy of living?

1932

Philosophers who say: "after death a timeless state will begin", or: "at death a timeless state begins", and do not notice that they have used the words "after" and "at" and "begins" in a temporal sense, and that temporality is embedded in their grammar.

Circa 1932–1934

Remember the impression one gets from good architecture, that it expresses a thought. It makes one want to respond with a gesture.

Spiele nicht mit den Tiefen des Andern!

Das Gesicht ist die Seele des Körpers.

Man kann den eigenen Charakter so wenig von Außen betrachten, wie die *eigene Schrift*. Ich habe zu meiner Schrift eine einseitige Stellung, die mich verhindert, sie auf gleichem Fuß mit anderen Schriften zu sehen und zu vergleichen.

In der Kunst ist es schwer etwas zu sagen, was so gut ist wie: nichts zu sagen.

An meinem Denken, wie an dem jedes Menschen, hängen die verdorrten Reste meiner früheren (abgestorbenen) Gedanken.

Die musikalische *Gedankenstärke* bei Brahms.

Die verschiedenen Pflanzen und ihr menschlicher Charakter: Rose, Epheu, Gras, Eiche, Apfelbaum, Getreide, Palme. Verglichen mit dem verschiedenen Charakter der Wörter.

Wenn man das Wesen der Mendelssohnschen Musik charakterisieren wollte, so könnte man es dadurch tun, daß man sagte, es gäbe vielleicht keine schwer verständliche Mendelssohnsche Musik.

Jeder Künstler ist von Andern beeinflußt worden und zeigt die Spuren dieser Beeinflussung in seinen Werken; aber was er uns bedeutet, ist doch nur *seine* Persönlichkeit. Was vom Andern stammt, können nur Eierschalen sein. Daß sie da sind, mögen wir mit Nachsicht behandeln, aber unsere geistige Nahrung werden sie nicht sein.

Es kommt mir manchmal vor, als philosophierte ich bereits mit einem zahnlosen Mund und als schiene mir das Sprechen mit einem zahnlosen Mund als das eigentliche, wertvollere. Bei Kraus sehe ich etwas Ähnliches. Statt, daß ich es als Verfall erkennte.

Don't play with what lies deep in another person!

The face is the soul of the body.

It is as impossible to view one's own character from outside as it is *one's own handwriting*. I have a one-sided relation to my handwriting which prevents me from seeing it on the same footing as others' writing and comparing it with theirs.

In art it is hard to say anything as good as: saying nothing.

My thinking, like everyone's, has sticking to it the shrivelled remains of my earlier (withered) ideas.

The *strength of the thoughts* in Brahms's music.

The human character of various plants· rose, ivy, grass, oak, appletree, corn, palm. Compared with the different characters words have.

If one wanted to characterize the essence of Mendelssohn's music, one could do it by saying that perhaps Mendelssohn wrote no music that is hard to understand.

Every artist has been influenced by others and shows traces of that influence in his works; but his significance for us is nothing but *his* personality. What he inherits from others can be nothing but egg-shells. We should treat their presence with indulgence, but they won't provide us with spiritual nourishment.

It sometimes seems to me as though I were already philosophizing with toothless gums and as though I took speaking without teeth for the right way, the more worthwhile way. I can detect something similar in Kraus. Instead of my recognizing that it's a deterioration.

1933

Wenn etwa jemand sagt »A's Augen haben einen schöneren Ausdruck als B's«, so will ich sagen, daß er mit dem Wort »schön« gewiß nicht dasjenige meint, was allem, was wir schön nennen, gemeinsam ist. Vielmehr spielt er ein Spiel von ganz geringem Umfang mit diesem Wort. Aber worin drückt sich das aus? Schwebte mir denn eine bestimmte enge Erklärung des Wortes »schön« vor? Gewiß nicht. – Aber ich werde vielleicht nicht einmal die Schönheit des Ausdrucks der Augen mit der Schönheit der Form der Nase vergleichen wollen.

Ja, man könnte etwa sagen: Wenn es in einer Sprache zwei Worte gäbe und also das Gemeinsame in diesem Falle nicht bezeichnet wäre, so würde ich für meinen Fall ruhig eines der beiden spezielleren Worte nehmen und es wäre mir nicht vom Sinn verloren gegangen.

Wenn ich sage, A. habe schöne Augen, so kann man mich fragen: was findest Du an seinen Augen schön, und ich werde etwa antworten: die Mandelform, die langen Wimpern, die zarten Lider. Was ist das Gemeinsame dieser Augen mit einer gothischen Kirche, die ich auch schön finde? Soll ich sagen, sie machen mir einen ähnlichen Eindruck? Wie, wenn ich sagte: das Gemeinsame ist, daß meine Hand versucht ist, sie beide nachzuzeichnen? Das wäre jedenfalls eine *enge Definition* des Schönen.

Man wird oft sagen können: frage nach den Gründen, warum Du etwas gut oder schön nennst, und die besondere Grammatik des Wortes ›gut‹ in diesem Fall wird sich zeigen.

1933–1934

Ich glaube meine Stellung zur Philosophie dadurch zusammengefaßt zu haben, indem ich sagte: Philosophie dürfte man eigentlich nur *dichten*. Daraus muß sich, scheint mir, ergeben, wie weit mein Denken der Gegenwart, Zukunft, oder der Vergangenheit angehört. Denn ich habe mich damit auch als einen bekannt, der nicht ganz kann, was er zu können wünscht.

Wenn man in der Logik einen Trick anwendet, wen kann man tricken, außer sich selbst?

Namen der Komponisten. Manchmal ist es die Projektionsmethode, die wir als gegeben betrachten. Wenn wir uns etwa fragen: Welcher Name würde den Charakter dieses Menschen treffen? Manchmal aber projizieren wir den

1933

If someone says, let's suppose, "A's eyes have a more beautiful expression than B's", then I should say that he is certainly not using the word "beautiful" to mean what is common to everything we call beautiful. On the contrary, he is playing a game with the word that has quite narrow bounds. But what shows this? Did I have in mind some particular, restricted explanation of the word "beautiful"? Certainly not. – But perhaps I shall not even feel like comparing the beauty of expression in a pair of eyes with the beauty in the shape of a nose.

So perhaps we might say: if there were a language with two words so that there were no reference to anything common to such cases, I should have no trouble about using one of these two special words for my case and my meaning would not be impoverished.

If I say A has beautiful eyes someone may ask me: what do you find beautiful about his eyes, and perhaps I shall reply: the almond shape, long eye-lashes, delicate lids. What do these eyes have in common with a gothic church that I find beautiful too? Should I say they make a similar impression on me? What if I were to say that in both cases my hand feels tempted to draw them? That at any rate would be a *narrow definition* of the beautiful.

It will often be possible to say: seek your reasons for calling something good or beautiful and then the peculiar grammar of the word 'good' in this instance will be evident.

1933–1934

I think I summed up my attitude to philosophy when I said: philosophy ought really to be written only as a *poetic composition*. It must, as it seems to me, be possible to gather from this how far my thinking belongs to the present, future or past. For I was thereby revealing myself as someone who cannot quite do what he would like to be able to do.

If you use a trick in logic, whom can you be tricking other than yourself?

Composers' names. Sometimes we treat the method of projection as given. When we ask for instance: What name would fit this man's character? But sometimes we project the character into the name and treat this as given. In

Charakter in den Namen und sehen diesen als das Gegebene an. So scheint es uns, daß die uns wohl bekannten großen Meister gerade die Namen haben, die zu ihrem Werk passen.

1934

Wenn Einer prophezeit, die künftige Generation werde sich mit diesen Problemen befassen und sie lösen, so ist das meist nur eine Art Wunschtraum, in welchem er sich für das entschuldigt, was er hätte leisten sollen, und nicht geleistet hat. Der Vater möchte, daß der Sohn das erreicht, was er nicht erreicht hat, damit die Aufgabe, die er ungelöst ließ, doch eine Lösung fände. Aber der Sohn kriegt eine *neue* Aufgabe. Ich meine: der Wunsch, die Aufgabe möge nicht unfertig bleiben, hüllt sich in die Voraussicht, sie werde von der nächsten Generation weitergeführt werden.

Das überwältigende *Können* bei Brahms.

Wer Eile hat, wird in einem Wagen sitzend unwillkürlich anschieben, obwohl er sich sagen kann, daß er den Wagen gar nicht schiebt.

Ich habe auch, in meinen künstlerischen Tätigkeiten, nur *gute Manieren.*

1936

Die seltsame Ähnlichkeit einer philosophischen Untersuchung (vielleicht besonders in der Mathematik) mit einer ästhetischen. (Z. B., was an diesem Kleid schlecht ist, wie es gehörte, etc.)

1934 oder 1937

In den Zeiten der stummen Filme hat man alle Klassiker zu den Filmen gespielt, aber nicht Brahms und Wagner.
    Brahms nicht, weil er zu abstrakt ist. Ich kann mir eine aufregende Stelle in einem Film mit Beethovenscher oder Schubertscher Musik begleitet denken und könnte eine Art Verständnis für die Musik durch den Film bekommen. Aber nicht ein Verständnis Brahmsscher Musik. Dagegen geht Bruckner zu einem Film.

that case we get the impression that the great masters we know so well have just the names which suit their work.

1934

When someone prophesies that the next generation will take up these problems and solve them, that is usually a sort of wishful thinking, a way of excusing himself for what he should have accomplished and hasn't. A father would like his son to succeed where he has not succeeded, so that the problem he has left unsolved shall find its solution after all. But his son will face a *new* problem. What I mean is: a wish for the task not to remain uncompleted wears the disguise of a prediction that the next generation will make progress with it.

Brahms's overwhelming *ability*.

If someone in a hurry is sitting in a car he will push involuntarily, however much he may tell himself that he is not pushing the car at all.

In my artistic activities I really have nothing but *good manners*.

1936

The queer resemblance between a philosophical investigation (perhaps especially in mathematics) and an aesthetic one. (E.g. what is bad about this garment, how it should be, etc.)

1934 or 1937

In the days of silent films all kinds of classical works were played as accompaniments, but not Brahms or Wagner.

Not Brahms, because he is too abstract. I can imagine an exciting scene in a film accompanied by Beethoven's or Schubert's music and might gain some sort of understanding of the music from the film. But this would not help me to understand Brahms's music. Bruckner on the other hand would go with a film.

1937

Wenn du ein Opfer bringst und dann darauf eitel bist, so wirst du mit samt deinem Opfer verdammt.

Das *Gebäude Deines Stolzes* ist abzutragen. Und das gibt furchtbare Arbeit.

In einem Tag kann man die Schrecken der Hölle erleben; es ist reichlich genug Zeit dazu.

Es ist ein großer Unterschied zwischen den Wirkungen einer Schrift, die man leicht fließend lesen kann und einer, die man schreiben, aber nicht *leicht* entziffern kann. Man schließt in ihr die Gedanken ein, wie in einer Schatulle.

Die größere ›Reinheit‹ der nicht auf die Sinne wirkenden Gegenstände, z. B., der Zahlen.

Das Licht der Arbeit ist ein schönes Licht, das aber nur dann wirklich schön leuchtet, wenn es von noch einem andern Licht erleuchtet wird.

»Ja, so ist es«, sagst Du, »denn so *muß* es sein!«
(Schopenhauer: der Mensch lebt eigentlich 100 Jahre lang.)
   »Natürlich, so muß es sein!« Es ist da, als habe man die *Absicht* eines Schöpfers verstanden. Man hat das *System* verstanden.
   Man fragt sich nicht ›Wie lange leben denn Menschen wirklich?‹, das erscheint jetzt als etwas Oberflächliches; sondern man hat etwas tiefer Liegendes verstanden.

Nur[1] so nämlich können wir unsere Behauptungen der Ungerechtigkeit – oder Leere unserer Behauptungen entgehen, indem wir das Ideal als das, was es *ist*, nämlich als Vergleichsobjekt – sozusagen als Maßstab – in unsrer Betrachtung ansehen statt als das Vorurteil, dem Alles konformieren *muß*. Hierin nämlich liegt der Dogmatismus, in den die Philosophie so leicht verfallen kann.

---

[1] Vgl. *Philosophische Untersuchungen* § 131.

1937

If you offer a sacrifice and are pleased with yourself about it, both you and your sacrifice will be cursed.

The *edifice of your pride* has to be dismantled. And that is terribly hard work.

The horrors of hell can be experienced within a single day; that's plenty of time.

A script you can read fluently works on you very differently from one that you can write, but not decipher *easily*. You lock your thoughts up in this as though in a casket.

The greater 'purity' of objects which don't affect the senses, numbers for instance.

The light work sheds is a beautiful light, which, however, only shines with real beauty if it is illuminated by yet another light.

"Yes, that's how it is," you say, "because that's how it *must* be!" (Schopenhauer: man's real life span is 100 years.)
    "Of course, that's how it must be!" It is just as though you have understood a creator's *purpose*. You have grasped the *system*.
    You do not ask 'But how long do men actually live?' which strikes you now as a superficial matter; whereas you have understood something more profound.

The[1] only way for us to guard our assertions against distortion – or avoid vacuity in our assertions, is to have a clear view in our reflections of what the ideal *is*, namely an object of comparison – a yardstick, as it were – instead of making a prejudice of it to which everything *has to* conform. For this is what produces the dogmatism into which philosophy so easily degenerates.

[1] Cf. *Philosophical Investigations*, I, § 131.

Was ist denn aber das Verhältnis einer Betrachtung wie der Spenglers und der meinen? Die Ungerechtigkeit bei Spengler: Das Ideal verliert nichts von seiner Würde, wenn es als Prinzip der Betrachtungsform hingestellt wird. Eine gute Meßbarkeit. —

In Macaulays Essays ist vieles ausgezeichnet; nur seine *Werturteile* über Menschen sind lästig und überflüssig. Man möchte ihm sagen: laß die Gestikulation! und sag nur, was Du zu sagen hast.

Beinahe ähnlich, wie man sagt, daß die alten Physiker plötzlich gefunden haben, daß sie zu wenig Mathematik verstehen, um die Physik bewältigen zu können, kann man sagen, daß die jungen Menschen heutzutage plötzlich in der Lage sind, daß der normale, gute Verstand für die seltsamen Ansprüche des Lebens nicht mehr ausreicht. Es ist alles so verzwickt geworden, daß, es zu bewältigen, ein ausnahmsweiser Verstand gehörte. Denn es genügt nicht mehr, das Spiel gut spielen zu können; sondern immer wieder ist die Frage: ist dieses Spiel jetzt überhaupt zu spielen und welches ist das rechte Spiel?

Die Lösung des Problems, das Du im Leben siehst, ist eine Art zu leben, die das Problemhafte zum Verschwinden bringt.
      Daß das Leben problematisch ist, heißt, daß Dein Leben nicht in die Form des Lebens paßt. Du mußt dann Dein Leben verändern, und paßt es in die Form, dann verschwindet das Problematische.
      Aber haben wir nicht das Gefühl, daß der, welcher nicht darin ein Problem sieht, für etwas Wichtiges, ja das Wichtigste, blind ist? Möchte ich nicht sagen, der lebe so dahin — eben blind, gleichsam wie ein Maulwurf, und wenn er bloß sehen könnte, so sähe er das Problem?
      Oder soll ich nicht sagen: daß, wer richtig lebt, das Problem nicht als *Traurigkeit*, also doch nicht problematisch, empfindet, sondern vielmehr als eine Freude; also gleichsam als einen lichten Äther um sein Leben, nicht als einen fraglichen Hintergrund.

Auch Gedanken fallen manchmal unreif vom Baum.

Es ist für mich wichtig, beim Philosophieren immer meine Lage zu verändern, nicht zu lange auf *einem* Bein zu stehen, um nicht steif zu werden.
      Wie, wer lange bergauf geht, ein Stückchen rückwärts geht, sich zu erfrischen, andre Muskeln anzuspannen.

But then how is a view like Spengler's related to mine? Distortion in Spengler: The ideal doesn't lose any of its dignity if it's presented as the principle determining the form of one's reflections. A sound measure. —

Macaulay's essays contain many excellent things; but his *value judgements* about people are tiresome and superfluous. One feels like saying to him: stop gesticulating! and just say what you have to say.

Earlier physicists are said to have found suddenly that they had too little mathematical understanding to cope with physics; and in almost the same way young people today can be said to be in a situation where ordinary common sense no longer suffices to meet the strange demands life makes. Everything has become so intricate that mastering it would require an exceptional intellect. Because skill at playing the game is no longer enough; the question that keeps coming up is: can this game be played at all now and what would be the right game to play?

The way to solve the problem you see in life is to live in a way that will make what is problematic disappear.
    The fact that life is problematic shows that the shape of your life does not fit into life's mould. So you must change the way you live and, once your life does fit into the mould, what is problematic will disappear.
    But don't we have the feeling that someone who sees no problem in life is blind to something important, even to the most important thing of all? Don't I feel like saying that a man like that is just living aimlessly – blindly, like a mole, and that if only he could see, he would see the problem?
    Or shouldn't I say rather: a man who lives rightly won't experience the problem as *sorrow*, so for him it will not be a problem, but a joy rather; in other words for him it will be a bright halo round his life, not a dubious background.

Ideas too sometimes fall from the tree before they are ripe.

I find it important in philosophizing to keep changing my posture, not to stand for too long on *one* leg, so as not to get stiff.
    Like someone on a long up-hill climb who walks backwards for a while so as to revive himself and stretch some different muscles.

Das Christentum ist keine Lehre, ich meine, keine Theorie darüber, was mit der Seele des Menschen geschehen ist und geschehen wird, sondern eine Beschreibung eines tatsächlichen Vorgangs im Leben des Menschen. Denn die ›Erkenntnis der Sünde‹ ist ein tatsächlicher Vorgang, und die Verzweiflung desgleichen und die Erlösung durch den Glauben desgleichen. Die, die davon sagen (wie Bunyan), beschreiben einfach, was ihnen geschehen ist, was immer einer dazu sagen will.

Wenn ich mir Musik vorstelle, was ich ja täglich und oft tue, so reibe ich dabei – ich glaube immer – meine oberen und unteren Vorderzähne rhythmisch an einander. Es ist mir schon früher aufgefallen, geschieht aber für gewöhnlich ganz unbewußt. Und zwar ist es, als würden die Töne meiner Vorstellung durch diese Bewegung erzeugt. Ich glaube, daß diese Art, im Innern Musik zu hören, vielleicht sehr allgemein ist. Ich kann mir natürlich auch ohne die Bewegung meiner Zähne Musik vorstellen, die Töne sind aber dann viel schemenhafter, viel undeutlicher, weniger prägnant.

Auch im Denken gibt es eine Zeit des Pflügens unde eine Zeit der Ernte.

Wenn man z. B. gewisse bildhafte Sätze als Dogmen des Denkens für die Menschen festlegt, so zwar, daß man damit nicht Meinungen bestimmt, aber den *Ausdruck* aller Meinungen völlig beherrscht, so wird dies eine sehr eigentümliche Wirkung haben. Die Menschen werden unter einer unbedingten, fühlbaren Tyrannei leben, ohne doch sagen zu können, sie seien nicht frei. Ich meine, daß die katholische Kirche es irgendwie ähnlich macht. Denn das Dogma hat die Form des Ausdrucks einer Behauptung, und es ist an ihm nicht zu rütteln, und dabei *kann* man jede praktische Meinung mit ihm in Einklang bringen; freilich manche leichter, manche schwerer. Es ist keine *Wand* die Meinung zu beschränken, sondern wie eine *Bremse*, die aber praktisch den gleichen Dienst tut; etwa als hängte man, um Deine Bewegungsfreiheit zu beschränken, ein Gewicht an Deinen Fuß. Dadurch nämlich wird das Dogma unwiderlegbar und dem Angriff entzogen.

Wenn ich für mich denke, ohne ein Buch schreiben zu wollen, so springe ich um das Thema herum; das ist die einzige mir natürliche Denkweise. In einer Reihe gezwungen, fortzudenken, ist mir eine Qual. Soll ich es nun überhaupt probieren??
    Ich *verschwende* unsägliche Mühe auf ein Anordnen der Gedanken, das vielleicht gar keinen Wert hat.

Christianity is not a doctrine, not, I mean, a theory about what has happened and will happen to the human soul, but a description of something that actually takes place in human life. For 'consciousness of sin' is a real event and so are despair and salvation through faith. Those who speak of such things (Bunyan for instance) are simply describing what has happened to them, whatever gloss anyone may want to put on it.

When I imagine a piece of music, as I do often every day, I always, so I believe, grind my upper and lower teeth together rhythmically. I have noticed this before though I usually do it quite unconsciously. What's more, it's as though the notes I am imagining are produced by this movement. I believe this may be a very common way of imagining music internally. Of course I can imagine music without moving my teeth too, but in that case the notes are much ghostlier, more blurred and less pronounced.

Thinking too has a time for ploughing and a time for gathering the harvest.

The effect of making men think in accordance with dogmas, perhaps in the form of certain graphic propositions, will be very peculiar: I am not thinking of these dogmas as determining men's opinions but rather as completely controlling the *expression* of all opinions. People will live under an absolute, palpable tyranny, though without being able to say they are not free. I think the Catholic Church does something rather like this. For dogma is expressed in the form of an assertion, and is unshakable, but at the same time any practical opinion *can* be made to harmonize with it; admittedly more easily in some cases than in others. It is not a *wall* setting limits to what can be believed, but more like a *brake* which, however, practically serves the same purpose; it's almost as though someone were to attach a weight to your foot to restrict your freedom of movement. This is how dogma becomes irrefutable and beyond the reach of attack.

If I am thinking about a topic just for myself and not with a view to writing a book, I jump about all round it; that is the only way of thinking that comes naturally to me. Forcing my thoughts into an ordered sequence is a torment for me. Is it even worth attempting now?

I *squander* an unspeakable amount of effort making an arrangement of my thoughts which may have no value at all.

Leute sagen gelegentlich, sie könnten das und das nicht beurteilen, sie hätten nicht Philosophie gelernt. Dies ist ein irritierender Unsinn; denn es wird vorgegeben, die Philosophie sei irgendeine Wissenschaft. Und man redet von ihr etwa wie von der Medizin. – Das aber kann man sagen, daß Leute, die nie eine Untersuchung philosophischer Art angestellt haben, wie die meisten Mathematiker z. B., nicht mit den richtigen Sehwerkzeugen für derlei Untersuchung oder Prüfung ausgerüstet sind. Beinahe, wie Einer, der nicht gewohnt ist, im Wald nach Blumen, Beeren oder Kräutern zu suchen, keine findet, weil sein Auge für sie nicht geschärft ist, und er nicht weiß, wo insbesondere man nach ihnen ausschauen muß. So geht der in der Philosophie Ungeübte an allen Stellen vorbei, wo Schwierigkeiten unter dem Gras verborgen liegen, während der Geübte dort stehenbleibt und fühlt, hier sei eine Schwierigkeit, obgleich er sie noch nicht sieht. – Und kein Wunder, wenn man weiß, wie lange auch der Geübte, der wohl merkt, hier liege eine Schwierigkeit, suchen muß, um sie zu finden.

Wenn etwas gut versteckt ist, ist es schwer zu finden.

Man kann von religiösen Gleichnissen sagen, sie bewegen sich am Rande des Abgrundes. Z. B., von der Allegorie B⟨unyan⟩'s. Denn wie, wenn wir bloß dazusetzen: »und alle diese Fallen, Sümpfe, Abwege, sind vom Herrn des Weges angelegt, die Ungeheuer, Diebe, Räuber von ihm geschaffen worden«? Gewiß, das ist nicht der Sinn des Gleichnisses! aber diese Fortsetzung liegt zu nahe! Sie nimmt dem Gleichnis, für Viele und für mich, seine Kraft.

Dann aber besonders, wenn dies – sozusagen – verschwiegen wird. Anders wäre es, wenn auf Schritt und Tritt offen gesagt würde: ›Ich brauche dies als Gleichnis, aber schau: hier stimmt es nicht‹. Dann hätte man nicht das Gefühl, daß man hintergangen wird, daß jemand versucht mich auf Schleichwegen zu überzeugen. Man kann Einem z. B. sagen: »Danke Gott für das Gute, was Du empfängst, aber beklage Dich nicht über das Übel: wie Du es natürlich tätest, wenn ein Mensch Dir abwechselnd Gutes und Übles widerfahren ließe.« Es werden Lebensregeln in Bilder gekleidet. Und diese Bilder können nur dienen, zu *beschreiben*, was wir tun sollen, aber nicht dazu, es zu *begründen*. Denn um begründen zu können, dazu müßten sie auch weiter stimmen. Ich kann sagen: »Danke diesen Bienen für ihren Honig, als wären sie gute Menschen, die ihn für Dich bereitet haben«; das ist *verständlich* und beschreibt, wie ich wünsche, Du sollest Dich benehmen. Aber nicht: »Danke ihnen, denn sieh', wie gut sie sind!« – denn sie können Dich im nächsten Augenblick stechen.

Die Religion sagt: *Tu dies!* – *Denk so!* – aber sie kann es nicht begründen, und versucht sie es auch nur, so stößt sie ab; denn zu jedem Grund, den sie gibt, gibt es einen stichhaltigen Gegengrund. Überzeugender ist es, zu sagen: »Denke so! – so seltsam dies scheinen mag.« Oder: »Möchtest Du das nicht tun? – so abstoßend es ist.«

People sometimes say they cannot make any judgement about this or that because they have not studied philosophy. This is irritating nonsense, because the pretence is that philosophy is some sort of science. People speak of it almost as they might speak of medicine. – On the other hand we may say that people who have never carried out an investigation of a philosophical kind, like, for instance, most mathematicians, are not equipped with the right visual organs for this type of investigation or scrutiny. Almost in the way a man who is not used to searching in the forest for flowers, berries, or plants will not find any because his eyes are not trained to see them and he does not know where you have to be particularly on the lookout for them. Similarly, someone unpractised in philosophy passes by all the spots where difficulties are hidden in the grass, whereas someone who has had practice will pause and sense that there is a difficulty close by even though he cannot see it yet. – And this is no wonder for someone who knows how long even the man with practice, who realizes there is a difficulty, will have to search before he finds it.

When something is well hidden it is hard to find.

Religious similes can be said to move on the edge of an abyss. B⟨unyan⟩'s for example. For what if we simply add: "and all these traps, quicksands, wrong turnings, were planned by the Lord of the Road and the monsters, thieves and robbers were created by him"? Certainly, that is not the sense of the simile! But such a continuation is all too obvious! For many people, including me, this robs the simile of its power.

But more especially if this is – as it were – suppressed. It would be different if at every turn it were said quite honestly: 'I am using this as a simile, but look: it doesn't fit here.' Then you wouldn't feel you were being cheated, that someone was trying to convince you by trickery. Someone can be told for instance: "Thank God for the good you receive but don't complain about the evil: as you would of course do if a human being were to do you good and evil by turns." Rules of life are dressed up in pictures. And these pictures can only serve to *describe* what we are to do, not *justify* it. Because they could provide a justification only if they held good in other respects as well. I can say: "Thank these bees for their honey as though they were kind people who have prepared it for you"; that is *intelligible* and describes how I should like you to conduct yourself. But I cannot say: "Thank them because, look, how kind they are!" – since the next moment they may sting you.

Religion says: *Do this! – Think like that!* – but it cannot justify this and once it even tries to, it becomes repellent; because for every reason it offers there is a valid counter-reason. It is more convincing to say: "Think like this! however strangely it may strike you." Or: "Won't you do this? – however repugnant you find it."

Gnadenwahl: So darf man nur schreiben unter den fürchterlichsten Leiden –
und dann heißt es etwas ganz anderes. Aber darum darf dies auch niemand als
Wahrheit zitieren, es sei denn, er selbst sage es unter Qualen. – Es ist eben
keine Theorie. – Oder auch: Ist dies Wahrheit, so ist es nicht die, die damit
auf den ersten Blick ausgesprochen zu sein scheint. Eher als eine Theorie, ist es
ein Seufzer, oder ein Schrei.

Russell tat im Laufe unserer Gespräche oft den Ausspruch: »Logic's hell!« –
Und dies drückt *ganz* aus, was wir beim Nachdenken über die logischen
Probleme empfanden; nämlich ihre ungeheure Schwierigkeit, ihre Härte und
Glätte.

Der Hauptgrund dieser Empfindung war, glaube ich, das Faktum: daß jede
neue Erscheinung der Sprache, an die man nachträglich denken mochte, die
frühere Erklärung als unbrauchbar erweisen könnte. (Die Empfindung war,
daß die Sprache immer neue, und unmögliche, Forderungen heranbringen
konnte; und so jede Erklärung vereitelt wurde.)

Das aber ist die Schwierigkeit, in die Sokrates verwickelt wird, wenn er die
Definition eines Begriffes zu geben versucht. Immer wieder taucht eine
Anwendung des Wortes auf, die mit dem Begriff nicht vereinbar erscheint, zu
dem uns andere Anwendungen geleitet haben. Man sagt: es *ist* doch nicht so!
– aber es *ist* doch so! – und kann nichts tun, als sich diese Gegensätze beständig
zu wiederholen.

Die Quelle, die in den Evangelien ruhig und durchsichtig fließt, scheint in den
Briefen des Paulus zu *schäumen*. Oder, so scheint es *mir*. Vielleicht ist es eben
bloß meine eigene Unreinheit, die hier die Trübung hineinsieht; denn warum
sollte diese Unreinheit nicht das Klare verunreinigen können? Aber *mir* ist es,
als sähe ich hier menschliche Leidenschaft, etwas wie Stolz oder Zorn, was
sich nicht mit der Demut der *Evangelien* reimt. Als wäre hier *doch* ein Betonen
der eigenen Person, *und zwar als religiöser Akt*, was dem Evangelium fremd ist.
Ich möchte fragen – und möge dies keine Blasphemie sein –: »Was hätte wohl
Christus zu Paulus gesagt?« Aber man könnte mit Recht darauf antworten:
Was geht Dich das an? Schau, daß *Du* anständiger wirst! Wie Du bist, kannst
Du überhaupt nicht verstehen, was hier die Wahrheit sein mag.

In den Evangelien – so scheint mir – ist alles *schlichter*, demütiger, einfacher.
Dort sind Hütten; bei Paulus eine Kirche. Dort sind alle Menschen gleich und
Gott selbst ein Mensch; bei Paulus gibt es schon etwas wie eine Hierarchie;
Würden und Ämter. – So sagt quasi mein GERUCHSINN.

Laß uns menschlich sein. –

Predestination: It is only permissible to write like this out of the most dreadful suffering – and then it means something quite different. But for the same reason it is not permissible for someone to assert it as a truth, unless he himself says it in torment. – It simply isn't a theory. – Or, to put it another way: If this is truth, it is not the truth that seems at first sight to be expressed by these words. It's less a theory than a sigh, or a cry.

In the course of our conversations Russell would often exclaim: "Logic's hell!" – And this *perfectly* expresses the feeling we had when we were thinking about the problems of logic; that is to say, their immense difficulty, their hard and *slippery* texture.

I believe our main reason for feeling like this was the following fact: that every time some new linguistic phenomenon occurred to us, it could retrospectively show that our previous explanation was unworkable. (We felt that language could always make new, and impossible, demands; and that this made all explanation futile.)

But that is the difficulty Socrates gets into in trying to give the definition of a concept. Again and again a use of the word emerges that seems not to be compatible with the concept that other uses have led us to form. We say: but that *isn't* how it is! – it *is* like that though! and all we can do is keep repeating these antitheses.

The spring which flows gently and limpidly in the Gospels seems to have *froth* on it in Paul's Epistles. Or that is how it seems *to me*. Perhaps it is just my own impurity which reads turbidness into it; for why shouldn't this impurity be able to pollute what is limpid? But to me it's as though I saw human passion here, something like pride or anger, which is not in tune with the humility of the *Gospels*. It's as though he *is* insisting here on his own person, *and doing so moreover as a religious gesture*, something which is foreign to the Gospel. I want to ask – and may this be no blasphemy –: "What might Christ have said to Paul?" But a fair rejoinder to that would be: What business is that of yours? Attend to making *yourself* more honourable! In your present state you are quite incapable of understanding what may be the truth here.

In the Gospels – as it seems to me – everything is *less pretentious*, humbler, simpler. There you find huts; in Paul a church. There all men are equal and God himself is a man; in Paul there is already something like a hierarchy; honours and official positions. – That, as it were, is what my NOSE tells me.

Let us be human. –

〈Ich〉 nahm soeben Äpfel aus einem Papiersack, wo sie lange gelegen hatten; viele mußte ich zur Hälfte wegschneiden und wegwerfen. Als ich dann einen Satz von mir abschrieb, dessen letzte Hälfte schlecht war, sah ich ihn gleich als zur Hälfte faulen Apfel. Und so geht es mir überhaupt. Alles, was mir in den Weg kommt, wird in mir zum Bild dessen, worüber ich noch denke. (Ist dies eine gewisse Weiblichkeit der Einstellung?)

Mir geht es bei dieser Arbeit so, wie es Einem geht, wenn man sich vergebens anstrengt, einen Namen in die Erinnerung zu rufen; man sagt da: »denk an etwas Anderes, dann wird es Dir einfallen« – und so mußte ich immer wieder an Anderes denken, damit mir das einfallen konnte, wonach ich lange *gesucht* hatte.

Der Ursprung und die primitive Form des Sprachspiels ist eine Reaktion; erst auf dieser können die komplizierteren Formen wachsen.

Die Sprache – will ich sagen – ist eine Verfeinerung, ›im Anfang war die Tat‹.[1]

Kierkegaard schreibt: Wenn das Christentum so leicht und gemütlich wäre, wozu hätte Gott in seiner Schrift Himmel und Erde in Bewegung gesetzt, mit *ewigen* Strafen gedroht? – Frage: Warum aber ist dann diese Schrift so undeutlich? Wenn man jemand vor furchtbarer Gefahr warnen will, tut man es, indem man ihm ein Rätsel zu raten gibt, dessen Lösung etwa die Warnung ist? – Aber wer sagt, daß die Schrift wirklich undeutlich ist: ist es nicht möglich, daß es hier wesentlich war, ›ein Rätsel aufzugeben‹? Daß eine direktere Warnung dennoch die *falsche* Wirkung hätte haben müssen? Gott läßt das Leben des Gottmenschen von *vier* Menschen berichten, von jedem anders, und widersprechend – aber kann man nicht sagen: Es ist wichtig, daß dieser Bericht nicht mehr als sehr gewöhnliche historische Wahrscheinlichkeit habe, *damit* diese nicht für das Wesentliche, Ausschlaggebende gehalten werde. Damit der *Buchstabe* nicht mehr Glaube fände, als ihm gebührt und der *Geist* sein Recht behalte. D. h.: Was Du sehen sollst, läßt sich auch durch den besten, genauesten Geschichtsschreiber nicht vermitteln; *darum* genügt, ja ist vorzuziehen, eine mittelmäßige Darstellung. Denn, was Dir mitgeteilt werden soll, kann die auch mitteilen. (Ähnlich etwa, wie eine mittelmäßige Theaterdekoration besser sein kann, als eine raffinierte, gemalte Bäume besser als wirkliche, – die die Aufmerksamkeit von dem ablenken, worauf es ankommt.)

[1] Goethe: *Faust I.*

⟨I⟩ just took some apples out of a paper bag where they had been lying for a long time. I had to cut half off many of them and throw it away. Afterwards when I was copying out a sentence I had written, the second half of which was bad, I at once saw it as a half-rotten apple. And that's how it always is with me. Everything that comes my way becomes a picture for me of what I am thinking about at the time. (Is there something feminine about this way of thinking?)

In doing this work I find myself in a position like that of a man who is unsuccessfully struggling to recall a name; in such a case we say: "think of something else, then it will come to you" – and similarly I had constantly to think of something else so as to allow what I had been searching for for a long time to occur to me.

The origin and the primitive form of the language game is a reaction; only from this can more complicated forms develop.
   Language – I want to say – is a refinement, 'in the beginning was the deed'.[1]

Kierkegaard writes: If Christianity were so easy and cosy, why should God in his Scriptures have set Heaven and Earth in motion and threatened *eternal* punishments? – Question: But in that case why is this Scripture so unclear? If we want to warn someone of a terrible danger, do we go about it by telling him a riddle whose solution will be the warning? – But who is to say that the Scripture really is unclear? Isn't it possible that it was essential in this case to 'tell a riddle'? And that, on the other hand, giving a more direct warning would necessarily have had the *wrong* effect? God has *four* people recount the life of his incarnate Son, in each case differently and with inconsistencies – but might we not say: It is important that this narrative should not be more than quite averagely historically plausible *just so that* this should not be taken as the essential, decisive thing? So that the *letter* should not be believed more strongly than is proper and the *spirit* may receive its due. I.e. what you are supposed to see cannot be communicated even by the best and most accurate historian; and *therefore* a mediocre account suffices, is even to be preferred. For that too can tell you what you are supposed to be told. (Roughly in the way a mediocre stage set can be better than a sophisticated one, painted trees better than real ones, – because these might distract attention from what matters.)

[1] Goethe, *Faust*, Part I (In the Study).

Das Wesentliche, für Dein Leben Wesentliche, aber legt der Geist in diese Worte. Du SOLLST gerade nur das deutlich sehen, was auch *diese* Darstellung deutlich zeigt. (Ich weiß nicht sicher, wie weit dies alles genau im Geiste Kierkegaards ist.)

In der Religion müßte es so sein, daß jeder Stufe der Religiosität eine Art des Ausdrucks entspräche, die auf einer niedrigeren Stufe keinen Sinn hat. Für den jetzt auf der niedrigern Stufe Stehenden ist diese Lehre, die auf der höheren Bedeutung hat, null und nichtig; sie *kann* nur *falsch* verstanden werden, und dabei gelten diese Worte für diesen Menschen *nicht*.

Die Lehre, z. B., von der Gnadenwahl bei Paulus ist auf meiner Stufe Irreligiosität, ein häßlicher Unsinn. Daher gehört sie nicht für mich, da ich das mir gebotene Bild nur falsch anwenden kann. Ist es ein frommes und gutes Bild, dann für eine ganz andere Stufe, auf der es gänzlich anders im Leben muß angewandt werden, als ich es anwenden könnte.

Das Christentum gründet sich nicht auf eine historische Wahrheit, sondern es gibt uns eine (historische) Nachricht und sagt: jetzt glaube! Aber nicht, glaube diese Nachricht mit dem Glauben, der zu einer geschichtlichen Nachricht gehört, – sondern: glaube, durch dick und dünn und das kannst Du nur als Resultat eines Lebens. *Hier hast Du eine Nachricht, – verhalte Dich zu ihr nicht, wie zu einer anderen historischen Nachricht!* Laß sie eine *ganz andere* Stelle in Deinem Leben einnehmen. – Daran ist nichts *Paradoxes!*

Niemand kann mit Wahrheit von sich selbst sagen, daß er Dreck ist. Denn wenn ich es sage, so kann es in einem Sinne wahr sein, aber ich kann nicht selbst von dieser Wahrheit durchdrungen sein: sonst müßte ich wahnsinnig werden, oder mich ändern.

So sonderbar es klingt: Die historischen Berichte der Evangelien könnten, im historischen Sinn, erweislich falsch sein, und der Glaube verlöre doch nichts dadurch: aber *nicht*, weil er sich etwa auf ›allgemeine Vernunftwahrheiten‹ bezöge!, sondern, weil der historische Beweis (das historische Beweis-Spiel) den Glauben gar nichts angeht. Diese Nachricht (die Evangelien) wird glaubend (d. h. liebend) vom Menschen ergriffen. *Das* ist die Sicherheit dieses Für-wahr-haltens, nicht *Anderes*.

Der Glaubende hat zu diesen Nachrichten *weder* das Verhältnis zur historischen Wahrheit (Wahrscheinlichkeit), *noch* das zu einer Lehre von ›Vernunftwahrheiten‹. Das gibt's. – (Man hat ja sogar zu verschiedenen Arten dessen, was man Dichtung nennt, ganz verschiedene Einstellungen!).

The Spirit puts what is essential, essential for your life, into these words. The point is precisely that your are only SUPPOSED to see clearly what appears clearly even in *this* representation. (I am not sure how far all this is exactly in the spirit of Kierkegaard.)

In religion every level of devoutness must have its appropriate form of expression which has no sense at a lower level. This doctrine, which means something at a higher level, is null and void for someone who is still at the lower level; he *can* only understand it *wrongly* and so these words are *not* valid for such a person.

For instance, at my level the Pauline doctrine of predestination is ugly nonsense, irreligiousness. Hence it is not suitable for me, since the only use I could make of the picture I am offered would be a wrong one. If it is a good and godly picture, then it is so for someone at a quite different level, who must use it in his life in a way completely different from anything that would be possible for me.

Christianity is not based on a historical truth; rather, it offers us a (historical) narrative and says: now believe! But not, believe this narrative with the belief appropriate to a historical narrative, rather: believe, through thick and thin, which you can do only as the result of a life. *Here you have a narrative, don't take the same attitude to it as you take to other historical narratives!* Make a *quite different* place in your life for it. There is nothing *paradoxical* about that!

Nobody can truthfully say of himself that he is filth. Because if I do say it, though it can be true in a sense, this is not a truth by which I myself can be penetrated: otherwise I should either have to go mad or change myself.

Queer as it sounds: The historical accounts in the Gospels might, historically speaking, be demonstrably false and yet belief would lose nothing by this: *not*, however, because it concerns 'universal truths of reason'! Rather, because historical proof (the historical proof-game) is irrelevant to belief. This message (the Gospels) is seized on by men believingly (i.e. lovingly). *That* is the certainty characterizing this particular acceptance-as-true, not something *else*.

A believer's relation to these narratives is *neither* the relation to historical truth (probability), *nor yet* that to a theory consisting of 'truths of reason'. There is such a thing. – (We have quite different attitudes even to different species of what we call fiction!)

Ich lese: »Und niemand kann Jesum einen Herrn heißen, außer durch den heiligen Geist.« – Und es ist wahr: ich kann ihn keinen *Herrn* heißen; weil mir das gar nichts sagt. Ich könnte ihn ›das Vorbild‹, ja ›Gott‹ nennen – oder eigentlich: ich kann verstehen, wenn er so genannt wird; aber das Wort »Herr« kann ich nicht mit Sinn aussprechen. *Weil ich nicht glaube*, daß er kommen wird, mich zu richten; weil mir *das* nichts sagt. Und das könnte mir nur etwas sagen, wenn ich *ganz* anders lebte.

Was neigt auch mich zu dem Glauben an die Auferstehung Christi hin? Ich spiele gleichsam mit dem Gedanken. – Ist er nicht auferstanden, so ist er im Grab verwest, wie jeder Mensch. *Er ist tot und verwest.* Dann ist er ein Lehrer, wie jeder andere und kann nicht mehr *helfen*; und wir sind wieder verwaist und allein. Und können uns mit der Weisheit und Spekulation begnügen. Wir sind gleichsam in einer Hölle, wo wir nur träumen können, und vom Himmel, durch eine Decke gleichsam, abgeschlossen. Wenn ich aber WIRKLICH erlöst werden soll, – so brauche ich *Gewißheit* – nicht Weisheit, Träume, Spekulation – und diese Gewißheit ist der Glaube. Und der Glaube ist Glaube an das, was mein *Herz*, meine *Seele* braucht, nicht mein spekulierender Verstand. Denn meine Seele, mit ihren Leidenschaften, gleichsam mit ihrem Fleisch und Blut, muß erlöst werden, nicht mein abstrakter Geist. Man kann vielleicht sagen: Nur die *Liebe* kann die Auferstehung glauben. Oder: Es ist die *Liebe*, was die Auferstehung glaubt. Man könnte sagen: Die erlösende Liebe glaubt auch an die Auferstehung; hält auch an der Auferstehung fest. Was den Zweifel bekämpft, ist gleichsam die *Erlösung*. Das Festhalten an *ihr* muß das Festhalten an diesem Glauben sein. Das heißt also: sei erst erlöst und halte an Deiner Erlösung (halte Deine Erlösung) fest – dann wirst Du sehen, daß Du an diesem Glauben festhältst. Das kann also nur geschehen, wenn Du dich nicht mehr auf die Erde stützst, sondern am Himmel hängst. Dann ist *alles* anders und es ist ›kein Wunder‹, wenn Du dann kannst, was Du jetzt nicht kannst. (Anzusehen ist freilich der Hängende wie der Stehende, aber das Kräftespiel in ihm ist ja ein ganz anderes und er kann daher ganz anderes tun, als der·Stehende.)

Es ist unmöglich wahrer über sich selbst zu schreiben, als man *ist*. Das ist der Unterschied zwischen dem Schreiben über sich und über äußere Gegenstände. Über sich schreibt man, so hoch man ist. Da steht man nicht auf Stelzen oder auf einer Leiter, sondern auf den bloßen Füßen.

1938

Freuds Idee: Das Schloß ist im Wahnsinn nicht zerstört, nur verändert; der alte Schlüssel kann es nicht mehr aufsperren, aber ein anders gebildeter Schlüssel könnte es.

I read: "No man can say that Jesus is the Lord, but by the Holy Ghost."[1] – And it is true: I cannot call him *Lord*; because that says nothing to me. I could call him 'the paragon', 'God' even – or rather, I can understand it when he is called thus; but I cannot utter the word "Lord" with meaning. *Because I do not believe* that he will come to judge me; because *that* says nothing to me. And it could say something to me, only if I lived *completely* differently.

What inclines even me to believe in Christ's Resurrection? It is as though I play with the thought. – If he did not rise from the dead, then he decomposed in the grave like any other man. *He is dead and decomposed*. In that case he is a teacher like any other and can no longer *help*; and once more we are orphaned and alone. So we have to content ourselves with wisdom and speculation. We are in a sort of hell where we can do nothing but dream, roofed in, as it were, and cut off from heaven. But if I am to be REALLY saved, – what I need is *certainty* – not wisdom, dreams or speculation – and this certainty is faith. And faith is faith in what is needed by my *heart*, my *soul*, not my speculative intelligence. For it is my soul with its passions, as it were with its flesh and blood, that has to be saved, not my abstract mind. Perhaps we can say: Only *love* can believe the Resurrection. Or: It is *love* that believes the Resurrection. We might say: Redeeming love believes even in the Resurrection; holds fast even to the Resurrection. What combats doubt is, as it were, *redemption*. Holding fast to *this* must be holding fast to that belief. So what that means is: first you must be redeemed and hold on to your redemption (keep hold of your redemption) – then you will see that you are holding fast to this belief. So this can come about only if you no longer rest your weight on the earth but suspend yourself from heaven. Then *everything* will be different and it will be 'no wonder' if you can do things that you cannot do now. (A man who is suspended looks the same as one who is standing, but the interplay of forces within him is nevertheless quite different, so that he can act quite differently than can a standing man)

You cannot write anything about yourself that is more truthful than you yourself are. That is the difference between writing about yourself and writing about external objects. You write about yourself from your own height. You don't stand on stilts or on a ladder but on your bare feet.

1938

Freud's idea: In madness the lock is not destroyed, only altered; the old key can no longer unlock it, but it could be opened by a differently constructed key.

[1] 1 *Corinthians*, 12. (Tr.)

Von einer Brucknerschen Symphonie kann man sagen, sie habe *zwei* Anfänge: den Anfang des ersten und den Anfang des zweiten Gedankens. Diese beiden Gedanken verhalten sich nicht wie Blutsverwandte zu einander, sondern wie Mann und Weib.

Die Brucknersche Neunte ist gleichsam ein *Protest* gegen die Beethovensche und dadurch wird sie erträglich, was sie als eine Art Nachahmung nicht wäre. Sie verhält sich zur Beethovenschen sehr ähnlich, wie der Lenausche Faust zum Goetheschen, nämlich der katholische Faust zum aufgeklärten, etc. etc.

Nichts ist so schwer, als sich nicht betrügen.

Longfellow:
> In the elder days of art,
> Builders wrought with greatest care
> Each minute and unseen part,
> For the gods are everywhere.

(Könnte mir als ein Motto dienen.)

Erscheinungen mit sprachähnlichem Charakter in der Musik oder Architektur. Die sinnvolle Unregelmäßigkeit – in der Gotik z. B. (mir schweben auch die Türme der Basiliuskathedrale vor). Die Musik Bachs ist sprachähnlicher als die Mozarts und Haydns. Die Rezitative der Bässe im vierten Satz der neunten Symphonie von Beethoven. (Vergleiche auch Schopenhauers Bemerkung über die *allgemeine* Musik zu einem *besonderen* Text.)[1]

Im Rennen der Philosophie gewinnt, wer am langsamsten laufen kann. Oder: der, der das Ziel zuletzt erreicht.

1939

Sich psychoanalysieren lassen ist irgendwie ähnlich vom Baum der Erkenntnis essen. Die Erkenntnis, die man dabei erhält, stellt uns (neue) ethische Probleme; trägt aber nichts zu ihrer Lösung bei.

---

[1] Schopenhauer: Zur Metaphysik der Musik, *Die Welt als Wille und Vorstellung*, Kapitel 39.

A Bruckner symphony can be said to have *two* beginnings: it begins once with the first idea and then again with the second idea. These two ideas stand to each other not as blood relations, but as man and wife.

Bruckner's Ninth is a sort of *protest* against Beethoven's and this makes it bearable in a way it would not be if it were a sort of imitation. It is related to Beethoven's Ninth very much as Lenau's Faust is to Goethe's, that is to say as the Catholic to the Enlightenment Faust, etc. etc.

Nothing is so difficult as not deceiving oneself.

Longfellow:
> In the elder days of art,
> Builders wrought with greatest care
> Each minute and unseen part,
> For the gods are everywhere.

(This could serve me as a motto.)

Phenomena akin to language in music or architecture. Significant irregularity – in Gothic for instance (I am thinking too of the towers of St. Basil's Cathedral). Bach's music is more like language than Mozart's or Haydn's. The recitatives on the double basses in the fourth movement of Beethoven's ninth symphony. (Compare too Schopenhauer's remark about universal music composed to a *particular* text.)[1]

In philosophy the winner of the race is the one who can run most slowly. Or: the one who gets there last.

1939

In a way having oneself psychoanalysed is like eating from the tree of knowledge. The knowledge acquired sets us (new) ethical problems; but contributes nothing to their solution.

---

[1] Schopenhauer: The Metaphysics of Music, *The World as Will and as Idea*, Chapter 39.

1939–1940

Was fehlt der Mendelssohnschen Musik? Eine ›mutige‹ Melodie?

Das alte Testament gesehen als der Körper ohne Kopf; das neue Testament: der Kopf; die Briefe der Apostel: die Krone auf dem Haupt.

Wenn ich an die Judenbibel denke, das alte Testament allein, möchte ich sagen: diesem Körper fehlt (noch) der Kopf. Diesen Problemen fehlt die Lösung. Diesen Hoffnungen die Erfüllung. Aber ich denke mir nicht notwendigerweise einen Kopf mit einer *Krone*.

Der Neid ist etwas Oberflächliches – d. h.: die typische Farbe des Neides reicht nicht tief – weiter unten hat die Leidenschaft eine andere Färbung. (*Das* macht den Neid, natürlich, nicht weniger real.)

Das Maß des Genies ist der Charakter, – wenn auch der Charakter an sich *nicht* das Genie ausmacht. Genie ist nicht ›Talent *und* Charakter‹, sondern Charakter, der sich in der Form eines speziellen Talents kundgibt. Wie ein Mensch aus Mut einem ins Wasser nachspringt, so schreibt ein anderer aus Mut eine Symphonie. (Dies ist ein schwaches Beispiel.)

Das Genie hat nicht mehr Licht als ein andrer, rechtschaffener Mensch – aber es sammelt dies Licht durch eine bestimmte Art von Linse in einen Brennpunkt.

Warum wird die Seele von eiteln Gedanken bewegt, – wenn sie doch eitel sind? Nun, sie *wird* von ihnen bewegt.

(Wie kann der Wind den Baum bewegen, wo er doch nur Luft ist? Nun, er *bewegt* ihn; und vergiß es nicht.)

Man *kann* nicht die Wahrheit sagen; wenn man sich noch nicht selbst bezwungen hat. Man *kann* sie nicht sagen; – aber nicht, weil man noch nicht gescheit genug ist.

Nur der kann sie sagen, der schon in ihr *ruht*; nicht der, der noch in der Unwahrheit ruht, und nur einmal aus der Unwahrheit heraus nach ihr langt.

Auf seinen Lorbeeren auszuruhen ist so gefährlich, wie auf einer Schneewanderung ausruhen. Du nickst ein, und stirbst im Schlaf.

1939–1940

What does Mendelssohn's music lack? A 'courageous' melody?

The Old Testament seen as the body without its head; the New Testament: the head; the Epistles of the Apostles: the crown on the head.

When I think of the Jewish Bible, the Old Testament on its own, I feel like saying: the head is (still) missing from this body. These problems have not been solved. These hopes have not been fulfilled. But I do not necessarily have to think of a head as having a *crown*.

Envy is a superficial thing – i.e.: the colour characteristic of envy does not go down deep – further down passion has a different colour. (*That*, of course, does not make envy any the less real.)

The measure of genius is character, – even though character on its own does not amount to genius. Genius is not 'talent *plus* character', but character manifesting itself in the form of a special talent. Just as one man will show courage by jumping into the water after someone, so another will show courage by writing a symphony. (This is a weak example.)

There is no more light in a genius than in any other honest man – but he has a particular kind of lens to concentrate this light into a burning point.

Why is the soul moved by idle thoughts? – After all they are idle. Well, it *is* moved by them.

(How can the wind move the tree when it's nothing but air? Well, it *does* move it; and don't forget it.)

No one *can* speak the truth; if he has still not mastered himself. He *cannot* speak it; – but not because he is not clever enough yet.

The truth can be spoken only by someone who is already *at home* in it; not by someone who still lives in falsehood and reaches out from falsehood towards truth on just one occasion.

Resting on your laurels is as dangerous as resting when you are walking in the snow. You doze off and die in your sleep.

Die ungeheure Eitelkeit der Wünsche zeigt sich dadurch, daß ich z. B. den Wunsch habe, ein schönes Schreibebuch sobald wie möglich vollzuschreiben. Ich habe *nichts* davon; ich wünsche es nicht etwa, weil es nur meine Produktivität anzeigt; es ist bloß das *Verlangen*, etwas schon Gewohntes recht bald los zu werden; obwohl ich ja, sobald ich es los geworden bin, ein neues anfangen werde und sich dasselbe wiederholen muß.

Schopenhauer, könnte man sagen, ist ein ganz *roher* Geist. D. h.: Er hat Verfeinerung, aber in einer gewissen Tiefe hört diese plötzlich auf, und er ist so roh, wie der Roheste. Dort, wo eigentliche Tiefe anfängt, hört die seine auf.
Man könnte von Schopenhauer sagen: er geht nie in sich.

Ich sitze auf dem Leben, wie der schlechte Reiter auf dem Roß. Ich verdanke es nur der Gutmütigkeit des Pferdes, daß ich jetzt gerade nicht abgeworfen werde.

Wenn die Kunst dazu dient, ›Gefühle zu erzeugen‹, ist, am Ende, ihre sinnliche Wahrnehmung auch unter diesen Gefühlen?

Meine Originalität (wenn das das richtige Wort ist) ist, glaube ich, eine Originalität des Bodens, nicht des Samens. (Ich habe vielleicht keinen eigenen Samen.) Wirf einen Samen in meinen Boden, und er wird anders wachsen, als in irgend einem andern Boden.
Auch die Originalität Freuds war, glaube ich, von dieser Art. Ich habe immer geglaubt – ohne daß ich weiß, warum – daß der eigentliche Same der Psychoanalyse von Breuer, nicht von Freud, herrührt. Das Samenkorn Breuers kann natürlich nur ganz winzig gewesen sein. *Mut* ist immer originell.

Die Menschen heute glauben, die Wissenschaftler seien da, sie zu belehren, die Dichter und Musiker etc., sie zu erfreuen. *Daß diese sie etwas zu lehren haben*; kommt ihnen nicht in den Sinn.

Das Klavierspielen, ein Tanz der menschlichen Finger.

Shakespeare, könnte man sagen, zeigt den Tanz der menschlichen Leidenschaften. Er muß daher objektiv sein, sonst würde er ja nicht den Tanz der

An example that shows how monstrously vain wishes are is the wish I have to fill a nice notebook with writing as quickly as possible. I get *nothing* at all from this; I don't wish it because, say, it will be evidence of my productivity; it is no more than a *craving* to rid myself of something familiar as soon as I can; although as soon as I have got rid of it I shall have to start a fresh one and the whole business will have to be repeated.

Schopenhauer is quite a *crude* mind, one might say. I.e. though he has refinement, this suddenly becomes exhausted at a certain level and then he is as crude as the crudest. Where real depth starts, his comes to an end.

One could say of Schopenhauer: he never searches his conscience.

I sit astride life like a bad rider on a horse. I only owe it to the horse's good nature that I am not thrown off at this very moment.

If art serves 'to arouse feelings' is, perhaps, perceiving it with the senses to be included amongst these feelings?

I believe that my originality (if that is the right word) is an originality belonging to the soil rather than to the seed. (Perhaps I have no seed of my own.) Sow a seed in my soil and it will grow differently than it would in any other soil.

Freud's originality too was like this, I think. I have always believed – without knowing why – that the real germ of psycho-analysis came from Breuer, not Freud. Of course Breuer's seed-grain can only have been quite tiny. *Courage* is always original.

People nowadays think that scientists exist to instruct them, poets, musicians, etc. to give them pleasure. The idea *that these have something to teach them* – that does not occur to them.

Piano playing, a dance of human fingers.

Shakespeare displays the dance of human passions, one might say. Hence he has to be objective; otherwise he would not so much display the dance of

menschlichen Leidenschaften zeigen – sondern etwa über ihn reden. Aber er zeigt sie uns im Tanz, nicht naturalistisch. (Diese Idee habe ich von Paul Engelmann.)

Auch im höchsten Kunstwerk ist noch etwas, was man ›Stil‹, ja auch, was man ›Manier‹ nennen kann. *Sie* haben weniger Stil, als das erste Sprechen eines Kindes.

1940

Das Verführerische der kausalen Betrachtungsweise ist, daß sie einen dazu führt, zu sagen: »Natürlich, – so mußte es geschehen.« Während man denken sollte: *so* und auf viele andere Weise, kann es geschehen sein.

Wenn wir die ethnologische Betrachtungsweise verwenden, heißt das, daß wir die Philosophie für Ethnologie erklären? Nein, es heißt nur, daß wir unsern Standpunkt weit draußen einnehmen, um die Dinge *objektiver* sehen zu können.

Dasjenige, wogegen ich mich wehre, ist der Begriff einer idealen Exaktheit, der uns sozusagen a priori gegeben wäre. Zu verschiedenen Zeiten sind unsere Ideale der Exaktheit verschieden; und keines ist das höchste.

Eine meiner wichtigsten Methoden ist es, mir den historischen Gang der Entwicklung unsrer Gedanken anders vorzustellen, als er in Wirklichkeit war. Tut man das, so zeigt uns das Problem eine ganz neue Seite.

Es ist oft nur sehr wenig unangenehmer die Wahrheit zu sagen, als eine Lüge; etwa nur so schwer wie bittern Kaffee zu trinken als süßen; und doch neige ich auch dann stark dazu, die Lüge zu sagen.

In aller großen Kunst ist eine WILDES Tier: *gezähmt.* Bei Mendelssohn, z. B., nicht. Alle große Kunst hat als ihren Grundbaß die primitiven Trieben des

human passions – as talk about it. But he displays it to us in a dance, not naturalistically. (I got this idea from Paul Engelmann.)

Even a work of supreme art has something that can be called 'style', something too that can even be called 'mannerism'. *They*[1] have less style than the first speech of a child.

1940

The insidious thing about the causal point of view is that it leads us to say: "Of course, it had to happen like that." Whereas we ought to think: it may have happened *like that* – and also in many other ways.

If we look at things from an ethnological point of view, does that mean we are saying that philosophy is ethnology? No, it only means that we are taking up a position right outside so as to be able to see things *more objectively*.

What I am opposed to is the concept of some ideal exactitude given us *a priori*, as it were. At different times we have different ideals of exactitude; and none of them is supreme.

One of the most important methods I use is to imagine a historical development for our ideas different from what actually occurred. If we do this we see the problem from a completely new angle.

Often it is only very slightly more disagreeable to tell the truth than to lie; about as difficult as drinking bitter rather than sweet coffee; and yet I still have a strong inclination to lie.

Within all great art there is a WILD animal: *tamed*. Not with Mendelssohn, for example. All great art has man's primitive drives as its groundbass. They are

---

[1] The manuscript gives no clue to the reference here. Rush Rhees plausibly suggests that Wittgenstein was thinking of Mannerist artists. The imitative character of Mannerism fits the comparison with a child's first attempt at speech. (Tr.)

Menschen. Sie sind nicht die *Melodie* (wie, vielleicht, bei Wagner), aber das, was der Melodie ihre *Tiefe* und Gewalt giebt.

In *diesem* Sinne kann man Mendelssohn einen ›*reproduktiven*‹ Künstler nennen. –

Im gleichen Sinn: mein Haus für Gretl[1] ist das Produkt entschiedener Feinhörigkeit, *guter* Manieren, der Ausdruck eines großen *Verständnisses* (für eine Kultur, etc.). Aber das *ursprüngliche* Leben, das *wilde* Leben, welches sich austoben möchte – fehlt. Man könnte also auch sagen, es fehlt ihm die *Gesundheit* (Kierkegaard). (Treibhauspflanze.)

Ein Lehrer, der während des Unterrichts gute, oder sogar erstaunliche Resultate aufweisen kann, ist darum noch kein guter Lehrer, denn es ist möglich, daß er seine Schüler, während sie unter seinem unmittelbaren Einfluß stehen, zu einer ihnen unnatürlichen Höhe emporzieht, ohne sie doch zu dieser Höhe zu entwickeln, so daß sie sofort zusammensinken, wenn der Lehrer die Schulstube verläßt. Dies gilt vielleicht von mir; ich habe daran gedacht. (Mahlers Lehranführungen[2] waren ausgezeichnet, wenn er sie leitete; das Orchester schien sofort zusammenzusinken, wenn er es nicht selbst leitete.)

›Zweck der Musik: Gefühle zu vermitteln.‹

Damit verbunden: Wir mögen mit Recht sagen »er hat jetzt das gleiche Gesicht wie früher« – obwohl die Messung in beiden Fällen Verschiedenes ergab.

Wie werden die Worte »der gleiche Gesichtsausdruck« gebraucht? – Wie weiß man, daß Einer diese Worte richtig gebraucht? Aber weiß ich, daß *ich* sie richtig gebrauche?

Man könnte sagen: »Genie ist *Mut im Talent.*«

Trachte geliebt und nicht-bewundert zu werden.

Not funk but funk conquered is what is worthy of admiration and makes life worth having been lived. Der Mut, nicht die Geschicklichkeit; nicht einmal die Inspiration, ist das Senfkorn, was zum großen Baum emporwächst. Soviel

---

[1] Wittgensteins Schwester, für die er das Haus Kundmanngasse 19, Wien gebaut hat.
[2] Unklare Stelle im Manuskript.

not the *melody* (as they are with Wagner, perhaps) but they are what gives the melody its *depth* and power.

In *this* sense Mendelssohn can be called a *'reproductive'* artist. –

In the same sense: the house I built for Gretl[1] is the product of a decidely sensitive ear and *good* manners, an expression of great *understanding* (of a culture, etc.). But *primordial* life, wild life striving to erupt into the open – that is lacking. And so you could say it isn't *healthy* (Kierkegaard). (Hothouse plant.)

A teacher may get good, even astounding, results from his pupils while he is teaching them and yet not be a good teacher; because it may be that, while his pupils are directly under his influence, he raises them to a height which is not natural to them, without fostering their own capacities for work at this level, so that they immediately decline again as soon as the teacher leaves the classroom. Perhaps this is how it is with me; I have sometimes thought so. (When Mahler himself conducted his students in training sessions[2] he obtained excellent performances; the orchestra seemed to deteriorate at once when he was not conducting it himself.)

'The aim of music: to communicate feelings.'

Connected with this: We may say correctly "his face has the same expression now as previously" – even though measurement yielded different results on the two occasions.

How do we use the words "the same facial expression"? – How do we know that someone is using these words correctly? But do I know that *I* am using them correctly?

One might say: "Genius is *talent exercised with courage*."

Aim at being loved without being admired.

Not funk but funk conquered is what is worthy of admiration and makes life worth having been lived. Courage, not cleverness; not even inspiration, – this is the grain of mustard that grows into a great tree. To the extent that there is

---

[1] Wittgenstein's sister, for whom he built the house at 19 Kundmanngasse, Vienna.
[2] The manuscript is unclear at this point.

Mut, soviel Zusammenhang mit Leben und Tod. (Ich dachte an Labors und Mendelssohns Orgelmusik.) Aber dadurch, daß man den Mangel an Mut in einem Andern einsieht, erhält man selbst nicht Mut.

Man muß manchmal einen Ausdruck aus der Sprache herausziehen, ihn zum Reinigen geben, – und kann ihn dann wieder in den Verkehr einführen.

Wie schwer fällt mir zu sehen, was *vor meinen Augen liegt!*

Du kannst nicht die Lüge nicht aufgeben wollen, und die Wahrheit sagen.

Den richtigen Stil schreiben heißt, den Wagen genau aufs Geleise setzen.

Wenn dieser Stein sich jetzt nicht bewegen will, wenn er eingekeilt ist, beweg' erst andre Steine, um ihn herum. –
Wir wollen Dich nur richtig auf die Bahn setzen, wenn Dein Wagen schief auf den Schienen steht. Fahren lassen wir Dich dann allein.

Mörtel abkratzen ist viel leichter, als einen Stein zu bewegen. Nun, man muß das Erste tun, bis man einmal das Andre tun kann.

1941

Mein Stil gleicht schlechtem musikalischen Satz.

Entschuldige nichts, verwische nichts, sieh und sag, wie es wirklich ist – aber Du mußt das sehen, was ein neues Licht auf die Tatsachen wirft.

Unsere größten Dummheiten können sehr weise sein.

Es ist unglaublich, wie eine neue Lade, an geeignetem Ort in unserem filing-cabinet, hilft.

courage there is a link with life and death. (I was thinking of Labor's and Mendelssohn's organ music.) But you don't win courage for yourself by recognizing the want of it in someone else.

Sometimes an expression has to be withdrawn from language and sent for cleaning, – then it can be put back into circulation.

How hard I find it to see what is *right in front of my eyes!*

You can't be reluctant to give up your lie, and still tell the truth.

Writing in the right style is setting the carriage straight on the rails.

If this stone won't budge at present and is wedged in, move some of the other stones round it first. –
    All we want to do is straighten you up on the track if your coach is crooked on the rails. Driving it afterwards is something we shall leave to you.

Scraping away mortar is much easier than moving a stone. Well, you have to do one before you can do the other.

1941

My style is like bad musical composition.

Don't apologize for anything, don't leave anything out; look and say what it's really like – but you must see something that throws new light on the facts.

Our greatest stupidities may be very wise.

It is incredible how helpful a new drawer can be, suitably located in our filing cabinet.

Du mußt Neues sagen und doch lauter Altes.

Du mußt allerdings nur Altes sagen – aber *doch* etwas Neues!

Die verschiedenen ›Auffassungen‹ müssen verschiedenen Anwendungen entsprechen.

Auch der Dichter muß sich immer fragen: ›ist denn, was ich schreibe, wirklich wahr?‹ – was nicht heißen muß: ›geschieht es so in Wirklichkeit?‹

Du mußt freilich Altes herbeitragen. Aber zu einem *Bau*. –

Im Alter *entschlüpfen* uns wieder die Probleme, so wie in der Jugend. Wir können sie nicht nur nicht aufknacken, wir können sie auch nicht halten.

Welche seltsame Stellungnahme der Wissenschaftler –: »Das wissen wir noch nicht; aber es läßt sich wissen, und es ist nur eine Frage der Zeit, so wird man es wissen«! Als ob es sich von selbst verstünde. –

Ich könnte mir denken, daß Einer meinte, die Namen »Fortnum« und »Mason« paßten zusammen.

Fordere nicht zuviel, und fürchte nicht, daß Deine gerechte Forderung ins Nichts zerrinnen wird.

Die Menschen, die immerfort ›warum‹ fragen, sind wie die Touristen, die, im Baedeker lesend, vor einem Gebäude stehen und durch das Lesen der Entstehungsgeschichte etc. etc. daran gehindert werden, das Gebäude zu *sehen*.

Der Kontrapunkt könnte für einen Komponisten ein außerordentlich schwieriges Problem darstellen; das Problem nämlich: in welches Verhältnis soll *ich* mit *meinen* Neigungen mich zum Kontrapunkt stellen? Er mochte ein konventionelles Verhältnis gefunden haben, aber wohl fühlen, daß es nicht das *seine* sei. Daß die Bedeutung nicht klar sei, welche der Kontrapunkt für ihn haben *solle*. (Ich dachte dabei an Schubert; daran, daß er am Ende seines Lebens noch Unterricht im Kontrapunkt zu nehmen wünschte. Ich meine, sein Ziel sei vielleicht nicht gewesen, einfach mehr Kontrapunkt zu lernen, als vielmehr sein Verhältnis zum Kontrapunkt zu finden.)

You must say something new and yet it must all be old.

In fact you must confine yourself to saying old things – and *all the same* it must be something new!

Different interpretations must correspond to different applications.

A poet too has constantly to ask himself: 'but is what I am writing really true?' – and this does not necessarily mean: 'is this how it happens in reality?'.

Yes, you have got to assemble bits of old material. But into a *building*. –

As we get old, problems *slip from our fingers* again, as they used to when we were young. It isn't just that we can't crack them, we cannot even keep hold of them.

What a curious attitude scientists have –: "We still don't know that; but it is knowable and it is only a matter of time before we get to know it!" As if that went without saying. –

I could imagine someone thinking that the names "Fortnum" and "Mason" fitted each other.

Don't demand too much, and don't be afraid that what you demand justly will melt into nothing.

People who are constantly asking 'why' are like tourists who stand in front of a building reading Baedeker and are so busy reading the history of its construction, etc., that they are prevented from *seeing* the building.

Counterpoint might present an extraordinarily difficult problem for a composer; the problem namely: what attitude should *I*, given *my* propensities, adopt to counterpoint? He may have hit upon a conventionally acceptable attitude and yet still feel that it is not properly *his*. That it is not clear what counterpoint *ought* to mean to him. (I was thinking of Schubert in this connection; of his wanting to take lessons in counterpoint right at the end of his life. I think his aim may have been not so much just learning more counterpoint as determining where he stood in relation to it.)

Wagners Motive könnte man musikalische Prosasätze nennen. Und so, wie es
>gereimte Prosa< gibt, kann man diese Motive allerdings zur melodischen Form
zusammenfügen, aber sie ergeben nicht *eine* Melodie.

Und so ist auch das Wagnersche Drama kein Drama, sondern eine
Aneinanderreihung von Situationen, die wie auf einem Faden aufgefädelt
sind, der selbst nur *klug* gesponnen, aber nicht, wie die Motive und
Situationen, inspiriert ist.

Laß Dich nicht von dem Beispiel Anderer führen, sondern von der Natur!

Die Sprache der Philosophen ist schon eine gleichsam durch zu enge Schuhe
deformierte.

Die Personen eines Dramas erregen unsere Teilnahme, sie sind uns wie
Bekannte, oft wie Menschen, die wir lieben oder hassen: Die Personen im
zweiten Teil des >Fausts< erregen unsere Teilnahme gar nicht! Wir haben nie
die Empfindung, als kennten wir sie. Sie ziehen an uns vorüber, wie
Gedanken, nicht wie Menschen.

1942

Der Mathematiker (Pascal), der die Schönheit eines Theorems der Zah-
lentheorie bewundert; er bewundert gleichsam eine Naturschönheit. Es ist
wunderbar, sagt er, welch herrliche Eigenschaften die Zahlen haben. Es ist, als
bewunderte er die Regelmäßigkeiten einer Art von *Krystall*.

Man könnte sagen: welch herrliche Gesetze hat der Schöpfer in die Zahlen
gelegt!

Wolken kann man nicht *bauen*. Und darum wird die *erträumte* Zukunft nie
wahr.

Ehe man ein Flugzeug hatte, hat man Flugzeuge erträumt und wie die Welt
mit ihnen aussehen würde. Aber, wie die Wirklichkeit nichts weniger als
diesem Traume glich, so hat man überhaupt keinen Grund zu glauben, die
Wirklichkeit werde sich zu dem entwickeln, was man träumt. Denn unsre
Träume sind voll Tand, gleichsam Papiermützen und Kostüme.

Wagner's *motifs* might be called musical prose sentences. And just as there is such a thing as 'rhyming prose', so too these *motifs* can be joined together in melodic form, without their constituting *one* melody. Wagnerian drama too is not drama so much as an assemblage of situations strung together as though on a thread which, for its part, is merely *cleverly* spun and not inspired as the motifs and situations are.

Don't take the example of others as your guide, but nature!

Philosophers use a language that is already deformed as though by shoes that are too tight.

The characters in a drama excite our sympathy; they are like people we know, often like people we love or hate: the characters in the second part of 'Faust' don't arouse our sympathy at all! We never feel as though we knew them. They file past us like ideas, not like human beings.

1942

The mathematician (Pascal) who admires the beauty of a theorem in number theory; it's as though he were admiring a beautiful natural phenomenon. It's marvellous, he says, what wonderful properties numbers have. It's as though he were admiring the regularities in a kind of *crystal*.

One might say: what wonderful laws the Creator built into numbers!

You can't *build* clouds. And that's why the future you *dream* of never comes true.

Before aeroplanes existed people dreamed of aeroplanes and of what a world with them would look like. But just as the reality was not at all like what they dreamed, so we have no reason to think that the future will really develop in the way we dream now. For our dreams are covered in tinsel like paper hats and fancy dress costumes.

Die populär-wissenschaftlichen Schriften unsrer Wissenschaftler sind nicht der Ausdruck der harten Arbeit, sondern der Ruhe auf ihren Lorbeeren.

Wenn Du die Liebe eines Menschen *hast*, so kannst Du sie mit keinem Opfer überzahlen; aber jedes Opfer ist zu groß, um Dir sie zu *erkaufen*.

Förmlich wie es einen *tiefen* und einen seichten Schlaf gibt, so gibt es Gedanken, die tief im Innern vor sich gehen, und Gedanken, die sich an der Oberfläche herumtummeln.

Du kannst den Keim nicht aus dem Boden ziehen. Du kannst ihm nur Wärme und Feuchtigkeit und Licht geben und dann muß er wachsen. (Nur mit Vorsicht darfst Du ihn selbst *berühren*.)

Was hübsch ist, kann nicht schön sein. —

Ein Mensch ist in einem Zimmer *gefangen*, wenn die Tür unversperrt ist, sich nach innen öffnet; er aber nicht auf die Idee kommt zu *ziehen*, statt gegen sie zu drücken.

Bring den Menschen in die unrichtige Atmosphäre und nichts wird funktionieren, wie es soll. Er wird an allen Teilen ungesund erscheinen. Bring ihn wieder in das richtige Element, und alles wird sich entfalten und gesund erscheinen. Wenn er nun aber im unrechten Element ist? Dann muß er sich also damit abfinden, als Krüppel zu erscheinen.

Wenn Weiß zu Schwarz wird, sagen manche Menschen »Es ist im Wesentlichen noch immer dasselbe«. Und andere, wenn die Farbe um einen Grad dunkler wird, sagen »Es hat sich *ganz* verändert«.

Architektur ist eine *Geste*. Nicht jede zweckmäßige Bewegung des menschlichen Körpers ist eine Geste. Sowenig, wie jedes zweckmäßige Gebäude Architektur.

The popular scientific books by our scientists aren't the outcome of hard work, but are written when they are resting on their laurels.

If you already *have* a person's love no sacrifice can be too much to give for it; but any sacrifice is too great to *buy* it for you.

Virtually in the same way as there is a difference between *deep* and shallow sleep, there are thoughts which occur deep down and thoughts which bustle about on the surface.

You cannot draw the seed up out of the earth. All you can do is give it warmth and moisture and light; then it must grow. (You mustn't even *touch* it unless you use care.)

What is pretty cannot be beautiful. –

A man will be *imprisoned* in a room with a door that's unlocked and opens inwards; as long as it does not occur to him to *pull* rather than push it.

Put a man in the wrong atmosphere and nothing will function as it should. He will seem unhealthy in every part. Put him back into his proper element and everything will blossom and look healthy. But if he is not in his right element, what then? Well, then he just has to make the best of appearing before the world as a cripple.

If white turns into black some people say "Essentially it is still the same". And others, if the colour becomes one degree darker, say "It has changed *completely*".

Architecture is a *gesture*. Not every purposive movement of the human body is a gesture. And no more is every building designed for a purpose architecture.

Wir kämpfen jetzt gegen eine Richtung. Aber diese Richtung wird sterben, durch andere Richtungen verdrängt, dann wird man unsere Argumentation gegen sie nicht mehr verstehen; nicht begreifen, warum man all das hat sagen müssen.

Den Fehler in einem schiefen Raisonnement suchen und Fingerhut-Verstecken.

1943

Denk' Dir, jemand hätte vor 2000 Jahren die *Form*

erfunden und gesagt, sie werde einmal die Form eines Instruments der Fortbewegung sein.

Oder vielleicht: es hätte jemand den vollständigen *Mechanismus* der Dampfmaschine konstruiert, ohne irgendwelche Ahnung, daß, und wie, er als Motor zu benützen wäre.

Was Du für ein Geschenk hältst, ist ein Problem, das Du lösen sollst.

Genie ist das, was uns das Talent des Meisters vergessen macht.

Genie ist das, was uns das Geschick vergessen macht.

Wo das Genie dünn ist, kann das Geschick durchschauen. (Meistersinger Vorspiel.)

Genie ist das, was macht, daß wir das Talent des Meisters nicht sehen können.

Nur wo das Genie dünn ist, kann man das Talent sehen.

1944

Friede in den Gedanken. Das ist das ersehnte Ziel dessen, der philosophiert.

At present we are combating a trend. But this trend will die out, superseded by others, and then the way we are arguing against it will no longer be understood; people will not see why all this needed saying.

Looking for the fallacy in a fishy argument and hunt-the-thimble.

Suppose that 2000 years ago someone had invented the *shape*

and had said that one day it would be the shape of an instrument of locomotion.

Or perhaps: that someone had constructed the complete *mechanism* of a steam engine without having any idea that, or how, it could be used to drive anything.

What you are regarding as a gift is a problem for you to solve.

Genius is what makes us forget the master's talent.

Genius is what makes us forget skill.

Where genius wears thin skill may show through. (Overture to the Mastersingers.)

Genius is what prevents us from seeing the master's talent.

Only where genius wears thin can you see the talent.

Thoughts that are at peace. That's what someone who philosophizes yearns for.

Warum soll ich nicht Ausdrücke entgegen ihren ursprünglichen Gebrauch verwenden? Tut das z. B. nicht Freud, wenn er auch einen Angsttraum einen Wunschtraum nennt? Wo ist der Unterschied? In der wissenschaftlichen Betrachtung ist der neue Gebrauch durch eine *Theorie* gerechtfertigt. Und ist diese Theorie falsch, dann ist auch der neue, ausgedehnte Gebrauch aufzugeben. In der Philosophie aber sind es nicht wahre oder falsche Meinungen über Naturvorgänge, auf die sich der ausgedehnte Gebrauch stützt. Keine Tatsache rechtfertigt ihn, keine kann ihn stützen.

Man sagt uns: »Du verstehst doch diesen Ausdruck? Nun also, in der Bedeutung, die Du kennst, gebrauche auch ich ihn.« [Nicht: »... in *der* Bedeutung –«.] Also wäre die Bedeutung eine Aura, die das Wort mitbringt und in jederlei Verwendung herübernimmt.

Der Philosoph ist der, der in sich viele Krankheiten des Verstandes heilen muß, ehe er zu den Notionen des gesunden Menschenverstandes kommen kann.

Wenn wir im Leben vom Tod umgeben sind, so auch in der Gesundheit des Verstands vom Wahnsinn.[1]

Denken *wollen* ist eins; Talent zum Denken haben, ein Anderes.

Wenn etwas an der Freudschen Lehre von der Traumdeutung ist; so zeigt sie, in wie *komplizierter* Weise der menschliche Geist Bilder der Tatsachen macht.
   So kompliziert, so unregelmäßig ist die Art der Abbildung, daß man sie *kaum* mehr eine Abbildung nennen kann.

1944 oder später

Es wird schwierig sein, meiner Darstellung zu folgen: denn sie sagt Neues, dem doch die Eierschalen des Alten ankleben.

Circa 1941–1944

Ob es eine unerfüllte Sehnsucht ist, die einen Menschen wahnsinnig macht? (Ich dachte an Schumann, aber auch an mich.)

---

[1] Vgl. Anm. d. Hrsg. zur S. 302 in *Bemerkungen über die Grundlagen der Mathematik.* (Suhrkamp Ausgabe.)

Why shouldn't I apply words in ways that conflict with their original usage? Doesn't Freud, for example, do this when he calls even an anxiety dream a wish-fulfilment dream? Where is the difference? In a scientific perspective a new use is justified by a *theory*. And if this theory is false, the new extended use has to be given up. But in philosophy the extended use does not rest on true or false beliefs about natural processes. No fact justifies it. None can give it any support.

People say to us: "You understand this expression don't you? Well, I too am using it with the meaning you are familiar with." (Not: ". . . with *that* particular meaning –".) This is to treat meaning as a halo that the word carries round with it and retains in any sort of application.

A philosopher is a man who has to cure many intellectual diseases in himself before he can arrive at the notions of common sense.

If in life we are surrounded by death, so too in the health of our intellect we are surrounded by madness.[1]

Wanting to think is one thing; having a talent for thinking another.

If Freud's theory on the interpretation of dreams has anything in it, it shows how *complicated* is the way the human mind represents the facts in pictures
So complicated, so irregular is the way they are represented that we can *barely* call it representation any longer.

1944 or later

My account will be hard to follow: because it says something new but still has egg-shells from the old view sticking to it.

Circa 1941–1944

Is it some frustrated longing that makes a man mad? (I was thinking of Schumann, but of myself too.)

---

[1] Cf. Editor's note on p. 302 of *Remarks on the Foundations of Mathematics*, Second Edition.

Circa 1944

Revolutionär wird der sein, der sich selbst revolutionieren kann.

What's ragged should be left ragged.

A miracle is, as it were, a *gesture* which God makes. As a man sits quietly and then makes an impressive gesture, God lets the world run on smoothly and then accompanies the words of a saint by a symbolic occurrence, a gesture of nature. It would be an instance if, when a saint has spoken, the trees around him bowed, as if in reverence. – Now, do I believe that this happens? I don't.

The only way for me to believe in a miracle in this sense would be to be *impressed* by an occurrence in this particular way. So that I should say e.g.: »It was *impossible* to see these trees and not to feel that they were responding to the words.« Just as I might say »It is impossible to see the face of this dog and not to see that he is alert and full of attention to what his master is doing«. And I can imagine that the mere report of the *words* and life of a saint can make someone believe the reports that the trees bowed. But I am not so impressed.

When I came home I expected a surprise and there was no surprise for me, so, of course, I was surprised.

Menschen sind in dem Maße religiös, als sie sich nicht so sehr *unvollkommen*, als *krank* glauben.
     Jeder halbwegs anständige Mensche glaubt sich höchst unvollkommen, aber der religiöse glaubt sich *elend*.

Glaube Du! Es schadet nicht.

Glauben heißt, sich einer Autorität unterwerfen. Hat man sich ihr unterworfen, so kann man sie nun nicht, ohne sich gegen sie auflehnen, wieder in Frage ziehen und auf's neue glaubwürdig finden.

Ein Notschrei kann nicht größer sein, als der *eines* Menschen.
     Oder auch *keine* Not kann größer sein, als die, in der ein einzelner Mensch sein kann.
     Ein Mensch kann daher in unendlicher Not sein und also unendliche Hilfe brauchen.

Circa 1944

That man will be revolutionary who can revolutionize himself.

What's ragged should be left ragged.

A miracle is, as it were, a *gesture* which God makes. As a man sits quietly and then makes an impressive gesture, God lets the world run on smoothly and then accompanies the words of a saint by a symbolic occurrence, a gesture of nature. It would be an instance if, when a saint has spoken, the trees around him bowed, as if in reverence. – Now, do I believe that this happens? I don't.

 The only way for me to believe in a miracle in this sense would be to be *impressed* by an occurrence in this particular way. So that I should say e.g.: "It was *impossible* to see these trees and not to feel that they were responding to the words." Just as I might say "It is impossible to see the face of this dog and not to see that he is alert and full of attention to what his master is doing". And I can imagine that the mere report of the *words* and life of a saint can make someone believe the reports that the trees bowed. But I am not so impressed.

When I came home I expected a surprise and there was no surprise for me, so, of course, I was surprised.

People are religious to the extent that they believe themselves to be not so much *imperfect*, as *ill*.
 Any man who is half-way decent will think himself extremely imperfect, but a religious man thinks himself *wretched*.

Go on, believe! It does no harm.

Believing means submitting to an authority. Having once submitted, you can't then, without rebelling against it, first call it in question and then once again find it acceptable.

No cry of torment can be greater than the cry of one man.
 Or again, *no* torment can be greater than what a single human being may suffer.
 A man is capable of infinite torment therefore, and so too he can stand in need of infinite help.

Die christliche Religion ist nur für den, der unendliche Hilfe braucht, also nur für den, der unendliche Not fühlt.

Der ganze Erdball kann nicht in größerer Not sein als *eine* Seele.

Der christliche Glaube – so meine ich – ist die Zuflucht in dieser *höchsten* Not.

Wem es in dieser Not gegeben ist, sein Herz zu öffnen, statt es zusammenzuziehen, der nimmt das Heilmittel ins Herz auf.

Wer das Herz so öffnet im reuigen Bekenntnis zu Gott, öffnet es auch für die Anderen. Er verliert damit seine Würde als ausgezeichneter Mensch und wird daher wie ein Kind. Nämlich ohne Amt, Würde und Abstand von den Andern. Sich vor den Andern öffnen kann man nur aus einer besonderen Art von Liebe. Die gleichsam anerkennt, daß wir alle böse Kinder sind.

Man könnte auch sagen: Der Haß zwischen den Menschen kommt davon her, daß wir uns von einander absondern. Weil wir nicht wollen, daß der Andere in uns hineinschaut, weil es darin nicht schön ausschaut.

Man soll nun zwar fortfahren, sich seines Innern zu schämen, aber nicht sich seines vor den Mitmenschen zu schämen.

Größere Not kann nicht empfunden werden, als von Einem Menschen. Denn wenn sich ein Mensch verloren fühlt, so ist das die höchste Not.

Circa 1945

Worte sind Taten.[1]

Nur ein sehr unglücklicher Mensch hat das Recht einen Andern zu bedauern.

Man kann vernünftigerweise nicht einmal auf Hitler eine Wut haben; wieviel weniger auf Gott.

Wenn Leute gestorben sind, so sehen wir ihr Leben in einem versöhnlichen Licht. Sein Leben scheint uns durch einen Dunst abgerundet. Aber für *ihn* war's nicht abgerundet, sondern zackig und unvollständig. Für ihn gab es keine Versöhnung; sein Leben ist nackt und elend.

Es ist als hätte ich mich verirrt und fragte ich jemand nun den Weg nach Hause. Er sagt, er wird mich ihn führen und geht mit mir einen schönen

---

[1] Vgl. *Philosophische Untersuchungen*, § 546.

The Christian religion is only for the man who needs infinite help, solely, that is, for the man who experiences infinite torment.

The whole planet can suffer no greater torment than a *single* soul.

The Christian faith – as I see it – is a man's refuge in this *ultimate* torment.

Anyone in such torment who has the gift of opening his heart, rather than contracting it, accepts the means of salvation in his heart.

Someone who in this way penitently opens his heart to God in confession lays it open for other men too. In doing this he loses the dignity that goes with his personal prestige and becomes like a child. That means without official position, dignity or disparity from others. A man can bare himself before others only out of a particular kind of love. A love which acknowledges, as it were, that we are all wicked children.

We could also say: Hate between men comes from our cutting ourselves off from each other. Because we don't want anyone else to look inside us, since it's not a pretty sight in there.

Of course, you must continue to feel ashamed of what's inside you, but not ashamed of yourself before your fellow-men.

No greater torment can be experienced than One human being can experience. For if a man feels lost, that is the ultimate torment.

Circa 1945

Words are deeds.[1]

Only a very unhappy man has the right to pity someone else.

It isn't sensible to be furious even at Hitler; how much less so at God.

After someone has died we see his life in a conciliatory light. His life appears to us with outlines softened by a haze. There was no softening for *him* though, his life was jagged and incomplete. For him there was no reconciliation; his life is naked and wretched.

It is as though I had lost my way and asked someone the way home. He says he will show me and walks with me along a nice smooth path. This suddenly

---

[1] Cf. *Philosophical Investigations*, I, § 546.

ebenen Weg. Der kommt plötzlich zu einem Ende. Und nun sagt mein Freund: »Alles, was Du zu tun hast, ist jetzt noch von hier an den Weg nach Hause finden.«

1946

Sind *alle* Leute große Menschen? Nein. – Nun, wie kannst Du dann hoffen, ein großer Mensch zu sein! Warum soll Dir etwas zuteil werden, was Deinen Nachbarn nicht zuteil wird? Wofür?! – Wenn es nicht der *Wunsch* ist, reich zu sein, der Dich glauben macht, Du seist reich, so muß es doch eine Beobachtung, eine Erfahrung, sein, die Dir das zeigt! Und welche Erfahrung hast Du (außer der der Eitelkeit)? Nur die eines *Talents*. Und meine Einbildung, ich sei ein außerordentlicher Mensch, ist ja *viel* älter, als meine Erfahrung meines besonderen Talents.

Schubert ist irreligiös und schwermütig.

Von den Melodien Schuberts kann man sagen, sie seien voller *Pointen*, und das kann man von den Mozarts nicht sagen; Schubert ist barock. Man kann auf gewisse Stellen einer Schubertschen Melodie zeigen und sagen: siehst Du, das ist der Witz dieser Melodie, hier spitzt sich der Gedanke zu.
   Auf die Melodien der verschiedenen Komponisten kann man jenes Prinzip der Betrachtung anwenden: Jede Baumart sei in anderem *Sinne* ›Baum‹. D. h.: Laß Dich nicht irreführen dadurch, daß man sagt, alles dies seien Melodien. Es sind Stufen auf einem Weg, der von etwas, was Du keine Melodie nennen würdest, zu etwas führt, was Du auch keine nennen würdest. Wenn man bloß die Tonfolgen und den Wechsel der Tonarten ansieht, so erscheinen alle diese Gebilde allerdings in Koordination. Siehst Du aber das Feld an, in dem sie stehen (also ihre Bedeutung), so wird man geneigt sein, zu sagen: Hier ist die Melodie etwas ganz anderes als dort (sie hat hier einen andern Ursprung, spielt eine andere Rolle, u. a.).

Der Gedanke, der sich an's Licht arbeitet.

Die Bemerkung des Jukundus im ›Verlornen Lachen‹,[1] seine Religion bestünde darin: er wisse, – wenn es ihm jetzt gut geht, – sein Schicksal könne sich zum Schlechten wenden. Dies drückt eigentlich die gleiche Religion aus, wie das Wort »Der Herr hat's gegeben, der Herr hat's genommen«.

---

[1] Gottfried Keller: *Das verlorne Lachen.*

stops. And now my friend tells me: "All you have to do now is find your way home from here."

Are *all* men great? No. – Well then, how can you have any hope of being a great man! Why should something be bestowed on you that's not bestowed on your neighbour? To what purpose?! If it isn't your *wish* to be rich that makes you think yourself rich, it must be something you observe or experience that reveals it to you! And what do you experience (other than vanity)? Simply that you have a certain *talent*. And my conceit of being an extraordinary person has been with me *much* longer than my awareness of my particular talent.

Schubert is irreligious and melancholy.

Schubert's tunes can be said to be full of *climaxes*, and this can't be said of Mozart's; Schubert is baroque. You can point to particular places in a tune by Schubert and say: look, that is the point of this tune, this is where the thought comes to a head.

We can apply to the tunes by the various composers the principle: each species of tree is a 'tree' in a different *sense* of the word. That is, don't be misled by the fact that we say all these are tunes. They are stages along a path which leads from something you would not call a tune to something else that you would equally not call a tune. If you just look at the sequences of notes and changes of key all these entities seem to be on the same level. But if you look at the context in which they exist (and hence at their meaning), you will be inclined to say: In this case melody is something quite different from what it is in that one (amongst other things, here it has a different origin and plays a different role).

The thought working its way towards the light.

Jukundus remarks in *The Lost Laugh*[1] that his religion consists in his knowing – now, when things are going well for him – that his fate could take a turn for the worse. This is really an expression of the same religion as the saying "The Lord hath given, the Lord hath taken away".

---

[1] Gottfried Keller: *The Lost Laugh*.

Es ist schwer, sich recht zu verstehen, denn dasselbe, was man aus Größe und Güte tun *könnte*, kann man aus Feigheit oder Gleichgültigkeit tun. Man kann sich freilich so und so aus wahrer Liebe benehmen, aber auch aus Hinterlist und auch aus Kälte des Herzens. Sowie nicht alle Milde Güte ist. Und nur wenn ich in Religion untergehen könnte, könnten diese Zweifel schweigen. Denn nur Religion könnte die Eitelkeit zerstören und in alle Spalten dringen.

Wenn man vorliest und *gut* vorlesen will, begleitet man die Worte mit stärkeren Vorstellungen. Wenigstens ist es *oft* so. Manchmal aber [»Nach Korinthus von Athen ...«][1] ist es die Interpunktion, d. h., die genaue Intonation und die Länge der Pausen, auf die uns alles ankommt.

Es ist merkwürdig, wie schwer es fällt, zu glauben, was wir nicht selbst einsehen. Wenn ich z. B. bewundernde Äußerungen der bedeutenden Männer mehrerer Jahrhunderte über Shakespeare höre, so kann ich mich eines Mißtrauens nie erwehren, es sei eine Konvention gewesen, ihn zu preisen; obwohl ich mir doch sagen muß, daß es so nicht ist. Ich brauche die Autorität eines *Milton*, um wirklich überzeugt zu sein. Bei diesem nehme ich an, daß er unbestechlich war. – Damit meine ich aber natürlich nicht, daß nicht eine ungeheure Menge Lobes ohne Verständnis und aus falschen Gründen Shakespeare gespendet worden ist und wird, von tausend Professoren der Literatur.

Die Schwierigkeit *tief* fassen, ist das Schwere.
    Denn seicht gefaßt, bleibt sie eben die Schwierigkeit. Sie ist mit der Wurzel auszureißen; und das heißt, man muß auf neue Art anfangen, über diese Dinge zu denken. Die Änderung ist z. B. eine so entschiedene, wie die von der alchemistischen zur chemischen Denkungsweise. – Es ist die neue Denkweise, die so schwer festzulegen ist.
    Ist die neue Denkweise festgelegt, so verschwinden die alten Probleme; ja, es wird schwer, sie wieder zu erfassen. Denn sie sitzen in der Ausdrucksweise; und wird eine neue angezogen, so streift man die alten Probleme mit dem alten Gewand ab.

Die hysterische Angst, die die Öffentlichkeit jetzt vor der Atom-Bombe hat, oder doch ausdrückt, ist beinahe ein Zeichen, daß hier einmal wirklich eine

[1] Goethe, *Die Braut von Korinth*.

Understanding oneself properly is difficult, because an action to which one *might* be prompted by good, generous motives is something one may also be doing out of cowardice or indifference. Certainly, one may be acting in such and such a way out of genuine love, but equally well out of deceitfulness, or a cold heart. Just as not all gentleness is a form of goodness. And only if I were able to submerge myself in religion could these doubts be stilled. Because only religion would have the power to destroy vanity and penetrate all the nooks and crannies.

If you are reading something aloud and want to read *well*, you accompany the words with vivid images. At least it is *often* like that. But sometimes ["Towards Corinth from Athens . . ."][1] what matters is the punctuation, i.e. your precise intonation and the duration of your pauses.

It is remarkable how hard we find it to believe something that we do not see the truth of for ourselves. When, for instance, I hear the expression of admiration for Shakespeare by distinguished men in the course of several centuries, I can never rid myself of the suspicion that praising him has been the conventional thing to do; though I have to tell myself that this is not how it is. It takes the authority of a *Milton* really to convince me. I take it for granted that he was incorruptible. – But I don't of course mean by this that I don't believe an enormous amount of praise to have been, and still to be, lavished on Shakespeare without understanding and for the wrong reasons by a thousand professors of literature.

Getting hold of the difficulty *deep down* is what is hard.

Because if it is grasped near the surface it simply remains the difficulty it was. It has to be pulled out by the roots; and that involves our beginning to think about these things in a new way. The change is as decisive as, for example, that from the alchemical to the chemical way of thinking. The new way of thinking is what is so hard to establish.

Once the new way of thinking has been established, the old problems vanish; indeed they become hard to recapture. For they go with our way of expressing ourselves and, if we clothe ourselves in a new form of expression, the old problems are discarded along with the old garment.

The hysterical fear over the atom bomb now being experienced, or at any rate expressed, by the public almost suggests that at last something really salutary

---

[1] Goethe, *The Bride of Corinth*.

heilsame Erfindung gemacht worden ist. Wenigstens macht die Furcht den Eindruck einer wirklich wirksamen bittern Medizin. Ich kann mich des Gedankens nicht erwehren: wenn hier nicht etwas Gutes vorläge, würden die *Philister* kein Geschrei anheben. Aber vielleicht ist auch das ein kindischer Gedanke. Denn alles, was ich meinen kann, ist doch nur, daß die Bombe das Ende, die Zerstörung, eines gräßlichen Übels, der ekelhaften, seifenwäßrigen Wissenschaft, in Aussicht stellt. Und das ist freilich kein unangenehmer Gedanke; aber wer sagt, was auf eine solche Zerstörung *folgen* würde? Die Leute, die heute gegen die Erzeugung der Bombe reden, sind freilich der *Auswurf* der Intelligenz, aber auch das beweist nicht unbedingt, daß das zu preisen ist, was sie verabscheuen.

Der Mensch ist das beste Bild der menschlichen Seele.[1]

Menschen sind in vorigen Zeiten ins Kloster gegangen. Waren das etwa dumme, oder stumpfe Menschen? – Nun, wenn solche Leute solche Mittel ergriffen haben, um weiter leben zu können, kann das Problem nicht leicht sein!

Die Gleichnisse Shakespeares sind, *im gewöhnlichen Sinne*, schlecht. Sind sie also dennoch gut – und ob sie es sind, weiß ich nicht – so müssen sie ihr eigenes Gesetz sein. Ihr Klang könnte sie z. B. wahrscheinlich, und zur Wahrheit, machen.

Es könnte sein, daß bei Shakespeare die Leichtigkeit, die Selbstherrlichkeit das Wesentliche ist, daß man ihn also hinnehmen müßte, um ihn wirklich bewundern zu können, wie man die Natur, eine Landschaft z. B., hinnimmt.

Wenn ich darin Recht habe, so würde das heißen, daß der Stil des ganzen Werkes, ich meine, seiner gesamten Arbeit, hier das Wesentliche, und Rechtfertigende, ist.

Daß ich ihn *nicht* verstehe, wäre dann damit zu erklären, daß ich ihn nicht *mit Leichtigkeit* lesen kann. Nicht so, also, wie man eine herrliche Landschaft besieht.

Der Mensch sieht wohl, was er hat, aber nicht, was er ist. Was er ist, ist gleichsam wie seine Höhe über dem Meeresspiegel, die man meistens nicht ohne weiteres beurteilen kann. Und die Größe, oder Kleinheit, eines Werks hängt davon ab, wo der steht, der es gemacht hat.

Man kann aber auch sagen: Der ist nie groß, der sich selbst verkennt: der sich einen blauen Dunst vormacht.

---

[1] Vgl. *Philosophische Untersuchungen*, Teil II, Abschn. IV.

has been invented. The fright at least gives the impression of a really effective bitter medicine. I can't help thinking: if this didn't have something good about it the *philistines* wouldn't be making an outcry. But perhaps this too is a childish idea. Because really all I can mean is that the bomb offers a prospect of the end, the destruction, of an evil, – our disgusting soapy water science. And certainly that's not an unpleasant thought; but who can say what would come *after* this destruction? The people now making speeches against producing the bomb are undoubtedly the *scum* of the intellectuals, but even that does not prove beyond question that what they abominate is to be welcomed.

The human being is the best picture of the human soul.[1]

In former times people went into monasteries. Were they stupid or insensitive people? – Well, if people like that found they needed to take such measures in order to be able to go on living, the problem cannot be an easy one!

Shakespeare's similes are, *in the ordinary sense*, bad. So if they are all the same good – and I don't know whether they are or not – they must be a law to themselves. Perhaps, e.g. their ring gives them plausibility and truth.

It may be that the essential thing with Shakespeare is his ease and authority and that you just have to accept him as he is if you are going to be able to admire him properly, in the way you accept nature, a piece of scenery for example, just as it is.

If I am right about this, that would mean that the style of his whole work, I mean of all his works taken together, is the essential thing and what provides his justification.

My *failure* to understand him could then be explained by my inability to read him *easily*. That is, as one views a splendid piece of scenery.

A man can see what he has, but not what he is. What he is can be compared to his height above sea level, which you cannot for the most part judge without more ado. And the greatness, or triviality, of a piece of work depends on where the man who made it was standing.

But you can equally say: a man will never be great if he misjudges himself: if he throws dust in his own eyes.

[1] Cf. *Philosophical Investigations*, II, iv.

Welch ein kleiner Gedanke doch ein ganzes Leben füllen kann!

Wie man doch sein ganzes Leben lang dasselbe kleine Ländchen bereisen kann, und meinen, es gäbe nichts außer ihm!

Man sieht alles in einer merkwürdigen Perspektive (oder Projektion): das Land, was man unaufhörlich bereist, kommt einem ungeheuer groß vor; alle umgebenden Länder sieht man wie schmale Randgebiete.

Um in die Tiefe zu steigen, braucht man nicht weit reisen; ja, Du brauchst dazu nicht Deine nächste und gewöhnliche Umgebung verlassen.

Es ist sehr *merkwürdig*, daß man zu meinen geneigt ist, die Zivilisation – die Häuser, Straßen, Wagen, etc. – entfernten den Menschen von seinem Ursprung, vom Hohen, Unendlichen, u.s.f. Es scheint dann, als wäre die zivilisierte Umgebung, auch die Bäume und Pflanzen in ihr, billig eingeschlagen in Zellophan, und isoliert von allem Großen und sozusagen von Gott. Es ist ein merkwürdiges Bild, was sich einem da aufdrängt.

Meine ›Errungenschaft‹ ist sehr ähnlich der eines Mathematikers, der einen Kalkül erfindet.

Wenn die Menschen nicht manchmal Dummheiten machten, geschähe überhaupt nichts Gescheites.

Das rein Körperliche kann unheimlich sein. Vergleiche die Art und Weise, wie man Engel und Teufel darstellt. Was man »Wunder« nennt, muß damit zusammenhängen. Es muß sozusagen eine *heilige Gebärde* sein.

Wie Du das Wort »Gott« verwendest, zeigt nicht, *wen* Du meinst – sondern, was Du meinst.

Beim Stierkampf ist der Stier der Held einer Tragödie. Zuerst durch Schmerzen tollgemacht, stirbt er einen langen und furchtbaren Tod.

Ein Held sieht dem Tod in's Angesicht, dem wirklichen Tod, nicht bloß dem Bild des Todes. Sich in einer Krise anständig zu benehmen, heißt nicht einen Helden, gleichsam wie auf dem Theater, gut darstellen können, sondern es heißt dem Tod *selbst* in's Auge schauen können.

Denn der Schauspieler kann eine Menge Rollen spielen, aber am Ende muß er doch *selbst* als Mensch sterben.

How small a thought it takes to fill someone's whole life!

Just as a man can spend his life travelling around the same little country and think there is nothing outside it!

You see everything in a queer perspective (or projection): the country that you keep travelling round strikes you as enormously big; the surrounding countries all look like narrow border regions.

If you want to go down deep you do not need to travel far; indeed, you don't have to leave your most immediate and familiar surroundings.

It is very *remarkable* that we should be inclined to think of civilization – houses, trees, cars, etc. – as separating man from his origins, from what is lofty and eternal, etc. Our civilized environment, along with its trees and plants, strikes us then as though it were cheaply wrapped in cellophane and isolated from everything great, from God, as it were. That is a remarkable picture that intrudes on us.

My 'achievement' is very much like that of a mathematician who invents a calculus.

If people did not sometimes do silly things, nothing intelligent would ever get done.

The purely corporeal can be uncanny. Compare the way angels and devils are portrayed. So-called "miracles" must be connected with this. A miracle must be, as it were, a *sacred gesture*.

The way you use the word "God" does not show *whom* you mean – but, rather, what you mean.

In a bullfight the bull is the hero of a tragedy. Driven mad first by suffering, he then dies a slow and terrible death.

A hero looks death in the face, real death, not just the image of death. Behaving honourably in a crisis doesn't mean being able to act the part of a hero well, as in the theatre, it means rather being able to look death *itself* in the eye.

For an actor may play lots of different roles, but at the end of it all *he himself*, the human being, is the one who has to die.

Worin besteht es: einer musikalischen Phrase mit Verständnis folgen? Ein Gesicht mit dem Gefühl für seinen Ausdruck betrachten? Den Ausdruck des Gesichts eintrinken?

Denk an das Benehmen Eines, der das Gesicht mit Verständnis für seinen Ausdruck zeichnet. An das Gesicht, an die Bewegungen des Zeichnenden; – wie drückt es sich aus, daß jeder Strich, den er macht, von dem Gesicht diktiert wird, daß nichts an seiner Zeichnung willkürlich ist, daß er ein *feines* Instrument ist?

Ist denn das wirklich ein *Erlebnis*? Ich meine: kann man sagen, daß dies ein Erlebnis ausdrückt?

Noch einmal: Worin besteht es, einer musikalischen Phrase mit Verständnis folgen, oder, sie mit Verständnis spielen? Sieh nicht in Dich selbst. Frag Dich lieber, was Dich sagen macht, *der Andre* tue dies. Und *was* veranlaßt Dich, zu sagen, *er* habe ein bestimmtes Erlebnis? Ja, sagt man das überhaupt? Würde ich nicht eher vom Andern sagen, er habe eine Menge von Erlebnissen?

Ich würde wohl sagen, »Er erlebt das Thema intensiv«; aber bedenke, was davon der Ausdruck ist.

Da könnte man nur wieder meinen, das intensive Erleben des Themas ›bestünde‹ in den Empfindungen der Bewegungen etc., womit wir es begleiten. Und das scheint (wieder) eine beruhigende Erklärung. Aber hast Du irgendeinen Grund, zu glauben, es sei so? Ich meine, z. B., eine Erinnerung an diese Erfahrung? Ist diese Theorie nicht wieder bloß ein Bild? Nein, es ist nicht so: Die Theorie ist nur ein Versuch, die Ausdrucksbewegungen mit einer ›Empfindung‹ zu kuppeln.

Fragst Du: wie ich das Thema empfunden habe, – so werde ich vielleicht sagen »Als Frage« oder dergleichen, oder ich werde es mit Ausdruck pfeifen etc.

»Er erlebt das Thema intensiv. Es geht etwas in ihm vor, während er es hört.« Und *was*?

Weist das Thema auf nichts außer sich? Oh ja! Das heißt aber: – der Eindruck, den es mir macht, hängt mit Dingen in seiner Umgebung

What does it consist in: following a musical phrase with understanding? Contemplating a face with sensitivity for its expression? Drinking in the expression on the face?

Think of the demeanour of someone drawing a face in a way that shows understanding for its expression. Think of the sketcher's face, his movements; – what shows that every stroke he makes is dictated by the face, that nothing in his drawing is arbitrary, that he is a *finely tuned* instrument?

Is that really an *experience*? What I mean is: can this be said to express an experience?

Once again: what is it to follow a musical phrase with understanding, or to play it with understanding? Don't look inside yourself. Consider rather what makes you say of *someone else* that this is what he is doing. And *what* prompts you to say that *he* is having a particular experience? For that matter, do we actually ever say this? Wouldn't I be more likely to say of someone else that he's having a whole host of experiences?

Perhaps I would say, "He is experiencing the theme intensely"; but consider how this is manifested.

One might again get the idea that experiencing a theme intensely 'consists' in sensations of the movements, etc., with which we accompany it. And that (again) looks a soothing explanation. But do you have any reason to think it true? Such as, for instance, a recollection of this experience? Isn't this theory once again just a picture? In fact,[1] it's not like this: The theory is no more than an attempt to link up the expressive movements with a 'sensation'.

If you ask me: How did I experience the theme? – perhaps I shall answer "As a question" or something of the sort, or I shall whistle it with expression, etc.

"He is experiencing the theme intensely. Something is happening within him as he hears it." *What* exactly?

Doesn't the theme point to anything beyond itself? Oh yes! But this means: the impression it makes on me is connected with things in its environment –

---

[1] The sense of the passage strongly suggests that "Nein" was a slip of the pen for (perhaps) "Nun". (Tr.).

zusammen – z. B. mit der Existenz der deutschen Sprache und ihrer Intonation, das heißt aber mit dem ganzen Feld unsrer Sprachspiele.

Wenn ich z. B. sage: Es ist, als ob hier ein Schluß gezogen würde, als ob hier etwas bekräftigt würde, oder, als ob *dies* eine Antwort auf das Frühere wäre, – so setzt mein Verständnis eben die Vertrautheit mit Schlüßen, Bekräftigungen, Antworten, voraus.

Ein Thema hat nicht weniger einen Gesichtsausdruck, als ein Gesicht.

»Die Wiederholung ist *notwendig*.« Inwiefern ist sie notwendig? Nun singe es, so wirst Du sehen, daß ihm erst die Wiederholung seine ungeheure Kraft gibt. – Ist es uns denn nicht, als müsse hier eine Vorlage für das Thema in der Wirklichkeit existieren, und das Thema käme ihr nur dann nahe, entspräche ihr nur, wenn dieser Teil wiederholt würde? Oder soll ich die Dummheit sagen: »Es klingt eben schöner mit der Wiederholung«? (Da sieht man übrigens, welche dumme Rolle das Wort »schön« in der Aesthetik spielt). Und doch *ist* da eben kein Paradigma außerhalb des Themas. Und doch *ist* auch wieder ein Paradigma außerhalb des Themas: nämlich der Rhythmus unsrer Sprache, unseres Denkens und Empfindens. Und das Thema ist auch wieder ein *neuer* Teil unsrer Sprache, es wird in sie einverleibt; wir lernen eine neue *Gebärde*.

Das Thema ist in Wechselwirkung mit der Sprache.

Eines ist, in Gedanken säen, eines, in Gedanken ernten.

Die beiden letzten Takte des »Tod und Mädchen« Themas, das⌒; man kann zuerst verstehen, daß diese Figur konventionell, gewöhnlich, ist, bis man ihren tiefern Ausdruck versteht. D. h., bis man versteht, daß hier das Gewöhnliche sinnerfüllt ist.

»Lebt wohl!«

»Eine ganze Welt des Schmerzen liegt in diesen Worten.« Wie *kann* sie in ihnen liegen? – Sie hängt mit ihnen zusammen. Die Worte sind wie die Eichel, aus der ein *Eichbaum* wachsen kann.

Esperanto. Das Gefühl des Ekels, wenn wir ein *erfundenes* Wort mit erfundenen Ableitungssilben aussprechen. Das Wort ist kalt, hat keine Assoziationen und spielt doch ›Sprache‹. Ein bloß geschriebenes Zeichensystem würde uns nicht so anekeln.

Man könnte Gedanken Preise anheften. Manche kosten viel, manche wenig. Und womit zahlt man für Gedanken? Ich glaube: mit Mut.

for example, with the existence of the German language and its intonation, but that means with the whole range of our language games.

If I say for instance: here it's as though a conclusion were being drawn, here as though someone were expressing agreement, or as though *this* were a reply to what came before, – my understanding of it presupposes my familiarity with conclusions, expressions of agreement, replies.

A theme, no less than a face, wears an expression.

"The repeat is *necessary*." In what respect is it necessary? Well, sing it, and you will see that only the repeat gives it its tremendous power. – Don't we have an impression that a model for this theme already exists in reality and the theme only approaches it, corresponds to it, if this section is repeated? Or am I to utter the inanity: "It just sounds more beautiful with the repeat"? (There you can see by the way what an idiotic role the word "beautiful" plays in aesthetics.) Yet there just *is* no paradigm apart from the theme itself. And yet again there *is* a paradigm apart from the theme: namely, the rhythm of our language, of our thinking and feeling. And the theme, moreover, is a *new* part of our language; it becomes incorporated into it; we learn a new *gesture*.

The theme interacts with language.

Sowing ideas is one thing, reaping ideas another.

The last two bars of the "Death and the Maiden" theme, the ◠◡; it's possible to understand this at first as an ordinary, conventional figure before coming to understand its deeper expression. I.e. before coming to understand that what is ordinary is here filled with significance.

"Fare well!"

"A whole world of pain is contained in these words." How *can* it be contained in them? – It is bound up with them. The words are like an acorn from which an *oak tree* can grow.

Esperanto. The feeling of disgust we get if we utter an *invented* word with invented derivative syllables. The word is cold, lacking in associations, and yet it plays at being 'language'. A system of purely written signs would not disgust us so much.

You could attach prices to thoughts. Some cost a lot, some a little. And how does one pay for thoughts? The answer, I think, is: with courage.

Wenn das Leben schwer erträglich wird, denkt man an eine Veränderung der Lage. Aber die wichtigste und wirksamste Veränderung, die des eigenen Verhaltens, kommt uns kaum in den Sinn, und zu ihr können wir uns schwer entschließen.

Man kann einen Stil schreiben der, in der Form unoriginell ist – wie der meine – aber mit gut gewählten Wörtern; oder aber einen, dessen *Form* originell, aus dem Innern neu gewachsen, ist. (Und natürlich auch einen, der nur irgendwie aus alten Stücken zusammengestoppelt ist.)

Das Christentum sagt unter anderm, glaube ich, daß alle guten Lehren nichts nützen. Man müsse das *Leben* ändern. (Oder die *Richtung* des Lebens.)

Daß alle Weisheit kalt ist; und daß man mit ihr das Leben so wenig in Ordnung bringen kann, wie man Eisen *kalt* schmieden kann.

Eine gute Lehre nämlich muß einen nicht *ergreifen*; man kann ihr folgen, wie einer Vorschrift des Arztes. – Aber hier muß man von etwas ergriffen und umgedreht werden. – (D. h., so verstehe ich's.) Ist man umgedreht, dann muß man umgedreht *bleiben*.

Weisheit ist leidenschaftslos. Dagegen nennt Kierkegaard den Glauben eine *Leidenschaft*.

Die Religion ist sozusagen der tiefste ruhige Meeresgrund, der ruhig bleibt, wie hoch auch die Wellen oben gehen. ——

»Ich habe nie früher an Gott geglaubt« – das versteh' ich. Aber nicht: »Ich habe nie früher wirklich an Ihn geglaubt.«

Ich fürchte mich oft vor dem Wahnsinn. Hab ich irgend einen Grund anzunehmen, daß diese Furcht nicht sozusagen einer optischen Täuschung entspringt: ich halte irgend etwas für einen nahen Abgrund, was keiner ist? Die einzige *Erfahrung*, von der ich weiß, die dafür spricht, daß diese keine Täuschung ist, ist der Fall Lenaus. In seinem »Faust« nämlich finden sich Gedanken der Art, wie ich sie auch kenne. Lenau legt sie in den Mund Fausts, aber es sind gewiß seine eigenen über sich selbst. Das Wichtige ist, was Faust über seine *Einsamkeit*, oder *Vereinsamung* sagt.

Auch sein Talent kommt mir dem meinen ähnlich vor: Viel Spreu – aber einige *schöne* Gedanken. Die Erzählungen im »Faust« sind alle schlecht, aber die Betrachtungen oft wahr und groß.

If life becomes hard to bear we think of a change in our circumstances. But the most important and effective change, a change in our own attitude, hardly even occurs to us, and the resolution to take such a step is very difficult for us.

One's style of writing may be unoriginal in form – like mine – and yet one's words may be well chosen; or, on the other hand, one may have a style that's original in *form*, one that is freshly grown from deep within oneself. (Or again it may, of course, just be botched together anyhow out of old bits and pieces.)

I believe that one of the things Christianity says is that sound doctrines are all useless. That you have to change your *life*. (Or the *direction* of your life.)

It says that wisdom is all cold; and that you can no more use it for setting your life to rights than you can forge iron when it is *cold*.

The point is that a sound doctrine need not *take hold* of you; you can follow it as you would a doctor's prescription. – But here you need something to move you and turn you in a new direction. – (I.e. this is how I understand it.) Once you have been turned round, you must *stay* turned round.

Wisdom is passionless. But faith by contrast is what Kierkegaard calls a *passion*.

Religion is, as it were, the calm bottom of the sea at its deepest point, which remains calm however high the waves on the surface may be. –

"I never believed in God before" – that I understand. But not: "I never really believed in Him before."

I am often afraid of madness. Do I have any reason for assuming that this fear does not spring from, so to speak, an optical illusion: taking something to be an abyss right at my feet, when it's nothing of the sort? The only *experience* I know of that speaks for its not being an illusion is the case of Lenau. For his "Faust" contains thoughts of a kind I too am familiar with. Lenau puts them into Faust's mouth, but they are certainly his own thoughts about himself. The important thing is what Faust says of his *loneliness*, or *isolation*.

His talent too strikes me as similar to mine: A lot of froth – but a few *fine* thoughts. The narratives in his "Faust" are all bad, but the observations are often true and great.

Lenaus »Faust« ist in sofern merkwürdig, als es der Mensch hier nur mit dem Teufel zu tun hat. Gott rührt sich nicht.

Ich glaube, Bacon war kein *scharfer Denker*. Er hatte große, sozusagen breite, Visionen. Aber wer nur diese hat, der muß im Versprechen großartig, im Erfüllen ungenügend, sein.
Jemand könnte eine Flugmaschine *erdichten*, ohne es mit ihren Einzelheiten genau zu nehmen. Ihr Äußeres mag er sich sehr ähnlich dem eines richtigen Aeroplanes vorstellen, und ihre Wirkungen malerisch beschreiben. Es ist auch nicht klar, daß so eine Erdichtung wertlos sein muß. Vielleicht spornt sie Andere zu einer anderen Art von Arbeit an. – Ja, während diese, sozusagen von fern her, die Vorbereitungen treffen, zum Bauen eines Aeroplanes, der wirklich fliegt, beschäftigt Jener sich damit, zu träumen, wie dieses Aeroplan aussehen muß, und was er leisten wird. Über den Wert dieser Tätigkeiten ist damit noch *nichts* gesagt. Die des Träumers *mag* wertlos sein – und auch die andere.

Den Wahnsinn *muß* man nicht als Krankheit ansehen. Warum nicht als eine plötzliche – mehr oder *weniger* plötzliche – Charakteränderung?

Jeder Mensch ist (oder die Meisten sind) mißtrauisch, und vielleicht gegen die Verwandten mehr, als gegen Andere. Hat das Mißtrauen einen Grund? Ja und nein. Man kann dafür Gründe angeben, aber sie sind nicht zwingend. Warum soll ein Mensch nicht plötzlich gegen die Menschen *viel* mißtrauischer werden? Warum nicht *viel* verschlossener? Oder liebeleer? Werden Menschen dies nicht auch im gewöhnlichen Verlauf? – Wo ist hier die Grenze zwischen Wollen und Können? *Will* ich mich niemandem mehr mitteilen, oder *kann* ich's nicht? Wenn so vieles seinen Reiz verlieren kann, warum nicht Alles? Wenn der Mensch auch im gewöhnlichen Leben verschlagen ist, warum soll er nicht – und *vielleicht* plötzlich – noch *viel* verschlagener werden? Und *viel* unzugänglicher.

Eine Pointe im Gedicht ist *überspitzt*, wenn die Verstandesspitzen nackt zu Tage treten, nicht überkleidet vom Herzen.

So, es kann ein Schlüssel für ewig da liegen, wohin ihn der Meister gelegt hat, und nie verwendet werden, das Schloß aufzusperren, dafür der Meister ihn geschmiedet hat.

Lenau's "Faust" is remarkable for the fact that man has dealings only with the Devil. God does not stir himself.

Bacon, in my view, was not a *precise thinker*. He had large-scale and, as it were, wide-ranging visions. But if this is all someone has, he is bound to be generous with his promises and inadequate when it comes to keeping them.

  Someone might *dream up* a flying machine without being precise about its details. He might imagine it as looking externally very much like a real aeroplane and describe its functioning graphically. Neither is it obvious that a phantasy like this must be worthless. Perhaps it will stimulate work of a different sort in others. – So while these others make preparations, a long time in advance as it were, to build an aeroplane that will really fly, he occupies himself with dreaming about what such an aeroplane will have to look like and what it will be capable of doing. This says *nothing* about the value of these activities. The dreamer's *may* be worthless – and so may the others'.

Madness need not be regarded as an illness. Why shouldn't it be seen as a sudden – more or *less* sudden – change of character?

Everybody is mistrustful (or most people are), perhaps more so towards their relations than towards others. Do they have any reason for mistrust? Yes and no. Reasons can be given, but they are not compelling. Why shouldn't a man suddenly become *much* more mistrustful towards others? Why not *much* more withdrawn? Or devoid of love? Don't people get like this even in the ordinary course of events? – Where, in such cases, is the line between will and ability? Is it that I *will* not open my heart to anyone any more, or that I *cannot*? If so much can lose its savour, why not everything? If people are wary even in ordinary life why shouldn't they – *perhaps* suddenly – become *much* more wary? And *much* more inaccessible?

An observation in a poem is overstated if the intellectual points are nakedly exposed, not clothed from the heart.

Yes, a key can lie for ever in the place where the locksmith left it, and never be used to open the lock the master forged it for.

»Es ist höchste Zeit, daß wir diese Erscheinungen mit etwas *anderem* vergleichen« – kann man sagen. – Ich denke da, z. B., an Geisteskrankheiten.

Freud hat durch seine phantastischen pseudo-Erklärungen (gerade weil sie geistreich sind) einen schlimmen Dienst erwiesen. (Jeder Esel hat diese Bilder nun zur Hand, mit ihrer Hilfe Krankheitserscheinungen zu ›erklären‹.)

Die Ironie in der Musik. Bei Wagner z. B. in den »Meistersingern«. Unvergleichlich tiefer im ersten Satz der IX. im Fugato. Hier ist etwas, was in der Rede dem Ausdruck grimmiger Ironie entspricht.

Ich hätte auch sagen können: das Verzerrte in der Musik. In dem Sinne, in dem man von gramverzerrten Zügen spricht. Wenn Grillparzer sagt, Mozart habe in der Musik nur das »Schöne« zugelassen, so heißt das, glaube ich, daß er nicht das Verzerrte, Gräßliche zugelassen habe, daß in seiner Musik sich nichts findet, was *diesem* entspricht. Ob das ganz wahr ist, will ich nicht sagen; aber angenommen, es ist so, so ist es ein Vorurteil Grillparzers, daß es von Rechts wegen nicht anders sein dürfe. Daß die Musik nach Mozart (besonders natürlich durch Beethoven) ihr Sprachgebiet erweitert hat, ist weder zu preisen, noch beklagen; sondern: *so hat sie sich gewandelt.* In Grillparzers Verhalten ist eine Art von Undankbarkeit. Wollte er *noch* einen Mozart haben? Konnte er sich etwas vorstellen, was so einer nun komponieren würde? Hätte er sich Mozart vorstellen können, wenn er ihn nicht gekannt hätte?
    Hier hat auch der Begriff »das Schöne« manchen Unfug angestellt.

Begriffe *können* einen Unfug erleichtern oder erschweren; begünstigen oder hemmen.

Die grinsenden Gesichter der Dummen können uns allerdings glauben machen, *sie* hätten kein wirkliches Leid; aber sie haben es, nur woanders als der Gescheitere. Sie haben, sozusagen, keinen *Kopf*schmerz, aber soviel anderes Elend, wie jeder Andere. Es muß ja nicht alles Elend, den *gleichen* Gesichtsausdruck hervorrufen. Ein edlerer Mensch in seinen Leiden wird anders ausschaun als ich.

"It is high time for us to compare these phenomena with something *different*"
– one may say. – I am thinking, e.g., of mental illnesses.

Freud's fanciful pseudo-explanations (precisely because they are brilliant)
perform a disservice.
   (Now any ass has these pictures available to use in 'explaining' symptoms of
illness.)

Irony in music. E.g. in Wagner's "Mastersingers". Incomparably deeper in
the Fugato in the first movement of the Ninth. There is something here
analogous to the expression of bitter irony in speech.

I could equally well have said: the distorted in music. In the sense in which we
speak of features distorted by grief. When Grillparzer says Mozart
countenanced only what is "beautiful" in music, I think he means that he did
not countenance what is distorted, frightful, that there is nothing corres-
ponding to *this* in his music. I am not saying that is completely true; but even
supposing it to be so, it is still a prejudice on Grillparzer's part to think that by
rights it ought not to be otherwise. The fact that music since Mozart (and of
course especially through Beethoven) has extended the range of its language is
to be neither commended nor deplored; rather: *this is how it has changed.* There
is something ungrateful about Grillparzer's attitude. Did he want *another*
Mozart? Could he imagine what such a being might have composed? Could
he have imagined Mozart if he had not known him?
   The concept of "the beautiful" has done a lot of mischief in this connection
too.

Concepts *may* alleviate mischief or they may make it worse; foster it or check
it.

We may perhaps think, looking at the grinning faces of idiots, that *they* do not
really suffer; they do though, only not in the same place as the more
intelligent. They do not have *head*ache, as it were, but as much suffering of
other sorts as anyone else. Not all suffering need after all evoke the *same* facial
expression. A nobler man will bear himself differently in affliction than I.

Ich kann nicht niederknien, zu beten, weil gleichsam meine Knie steif sind. Ich fürchte mich vor der Auflösung (vor meiner Auflösung), wenn ich weich würde.

Ich zeige meinen Schülern Ausschnitte aus einer ungeheuern Landschaft, in der sie sich unmöglich auskennen können.

1947

Die apokalyptische Ansicht der Welt ist eigentlich die, daß sich die Dinge *nicht* wiederholen. Es ist z. B. nicht unsinnig, zu glauben, daß das wissenschaftliche und technische Zeitalter der Anfang vom Ende der Menschheit ist; daß die Idee vom großen Fortschritt eine Verblendung ist, wie auch von der endlichen Erkenntnis der Wahrheit; daß an der wissenschaftlichen Erkenntnis nichts Gutes oder Wünschenswertes ist und daß die Menschheit, die nach ihr strebt, in eine Falle läuft. Es ist durchaus nicht klar, daß dies nicht so ist.

Was ein Mann träumt, das erfüllt sich so gut wie nie.

Sokrates, der den Sophisten immer zum Schweigen bringt – bringt er ihn *mit Recht* zum Schweigen? – Ja, der Sophist weiß nicht, was er zu wissen glaubte; aber das ist kein Triumph für Sokrates. Weder kann es heißen »Sieh da! Du weißt es nicht!« – noch, triumphierend, »Also wissen wir Alle nichts!«

Die Weisheit ist etwas Kaltes, und insofern Dummes. (Der Glaube dagegen, eine Leidenschaft.) Man könnte auch sagen: Die Weisheit *verhehlt* Dir nur das Leben. (Die Weisheit ist wie kalte, graue Asche, die die Glut verdeckt.)

Scheue Dich *ja* nicht davor, Unsinn zu reden! Nur mußt Du auf Deinen Unsinn lauschen.

Die Wunder der Natur.
    Man könnte sagen: die Kunst *zeige* uns die Wunder der Natur. Sie basiert auf dem *Begriff* der Wunder der Natur. (Die sich öffnende Blüte. Was ist an ihr *herrlich*?) Man sagt: »Sieh, wie sie sich öffnet!«

I cannot kneel to pray because it's as though my knees were stiff. I am afraid of dissolution (of my own dissolution), should I become soft.

I am showing my pupils details of an immense landscape which they cannot possibly know their way around.

1947

The truly apocalyptic view of the world is that things do *not* repeat themselves. It isn't absurd, e.g., to believe that the age of science and technology is the beginning of the end for humanity; that the idea of great progress is a delusion, along with the idea that the truth will ultimately be known; that there is nothing good or desirable about scientific knowledge and that mankind, in seeking it, is falling into a trap. It is by no means obvious that this is not how things are.

A man's dreams are virtually never realized.

Socrates keeps reducing the sophist to silence, – but does he have *right* on his side when he does this? Well, it is true that the sophist does not know what he thinks he knows; but that is no triumph for Socrates. It can't be a case of "You see! You don't know it!" – nor yet, triumphantly, of "So none of us knows anything!".

Wisdom is cold and to that extent stupid. (Faith on the other hand is a passion.) It might also be said: Wisdom merely *conceals* life from you. (Wisdom is like cold grey ash, covering up the glowing embers.)

Don't *for heaven's sake*, be afraid of talking nonsense! But you must pay attention to your nonsense.

The miracles of nature.
    One might say: art *shows* us the miracles of nature. It is based on the *concept* of the miracles of nature. (The blossom, just opening out. What is *marvellous* about it?) We say: "Just look at it opening out!"

Durch einen Zufall nur könnten die Träume eines Menschen von der Zukunft
der Philosophie, der Kunst, der Wissenschaft, sich bewahrheiten. Was er sieht,
ist eine Fortsetzung seiner Welt im Traum, also VIELLEICHT sein Wunsch
(vielleicht auch nicht), aber nicht die Wirklichkeit.

Auch der Mathematiker kann natürlich die Wunder (das Krystall) der Natur
anstaunen; aber kann er es, wenn es einmal problematisch geworden ist, *was* er
denn anschaut? Ist es wirklich möglich, solange eine philosophische Trübe das
verschleiert, was das Staunenswerte oder Angestaunte ist?
   Ich könnte mir denken, daß Einer Bäume bewundert, und auch die
Schatten, oder Spiegelungen von Bäumen, die er für Bäume hält. Sagt er sich
aber einmal, daß es doch keine Bäume sind und wird es für ihn problematisch,
was sie sind, oder was ihre Beziehung zu Bäumen ist, dann hat die
Bewunderung einen Riß, der erst zu heilen ist.

Manchmal kann ein Satz nur verstanden werden, wenn man ihn im *richtigen
Tempo* liest. Meine Sätze sind alle *langsam* zu lesen.

Die ›Notwendigkeit‹, mit der der zweite Gedanke auf den ersten folgt.
(Figaro Ouvertüre.) Nichts dümmer, als zu sagen, es sei ›angenehm‹ den einen
nach dem andern zu hören. – Aber das Paradigma, wonach das alles *richtig* ist,
ist freilich dunkel. ›Es ist die natürliche Entwicklung.‹ Man macht eine
Handbewegung, möchte sagen:»natürlich!« – Man könnte den Übergang
auch einem Übergang, dem Eintritt einer neuen Figur in einer Geschichte, z.
B., oder einem Gedichte, vergleichen. *So* paßt dies Stück in die Welt unsrer
Gedanken und Gefühle hinein.

Die Falten meines Herzens wollen immer zusammenkleben, und um es zu
öffnen müßte ich sie immer wieder auseinanderreißen.

Der amerikanische dumme und naive Film kann in aller seiner Dummheit und
durch sie belehren. Der trottelhafte, nicht-naive englische Film kann nicht
belehren. Ich habe oft aus einem dummen amerikanischen Film eine Lehre
gezogen.

Ist, was ich tue, überhaupt der Mühe wert? Doch nur, wenn es von oben her
ein Licht empfängt. Und ist es so, – warum sollte ich mich sorgen, daß mir die
Früchte meiner Arbeit nicht gestohlen werden? Wenn, was ich schreibe,

It could only be by accident that a man's dreams about the future of philosophy, art, science, should come true. What he sees in his dream is an extension of his own world, PERHAPS what he wishes (and perhaps not), but not reality.

The mathematician too can wonder at the miracles (the crystal) of nature of course; but can he do so once a problem has arisen about *what* it actually is he is contemplating? Is it really possible as long as the object that he finds astonishing and gazes at with awe is *shrouded* in a philosophical fog?

I could imagine somebody might admire not only real trees, but also the shadows or reflections that they cast, taking them too for trees. But once he has told himself that these are not really trees after all and has come to be puzzled at what they are, or at how they are related to trees, his admiration will have suffered a rupture that will need healing.

Sometimes a sentence can be understood only if it is read at the *right tempo*. My sentences are all supposed to be read *slowly*.

The 'necessity' with which the second idea succeeds the first. (The overture to "Figaro".) Nothing could be more idiotic than to say that it is *'agreeable'* to hear the one after the other. — All the same, the paradigm according to which everything is *right* is obscure. 'It is the natural development.' We gesture with our hands and are inclined to say: "Of course!" — Or we might compare the transition to a transition like the introduction of a new character in a story for instance, or a poem. *This* is how the piece fits into the world of our thoughts and feelings.

The linings of my heart keep sticking together and to open it I should each time have to tear them apart.

A typical American film, naïve and silly, can — for all its silliness and even *by means of* it — be instructive. A fatuous, self-conscious English film can teach one nothing. I have often learnt a lesson from a silly American film.

Is what I am doing really worth the effort? Yes, but only if a light shines on it from above. And if that happens — why should I concern myself that the fruits of my labours should not be stolen? If what I am writing really has some

wirklich wertvoll ist, wie sollte man mir das Wertvolle stehlen? Ist das Licht von oben *nicht* da, so kann ich ja doch nur geschickt sein.

Ich verstehe es vollkommen, wie Einer es *hassen* kann, wenn ihm die Priorität seiner Erfindung, oder Entdeckung, streitig gemacht wird, daß er diese Priorität ›with tooth and claw‹ verteidigen möchte. *Und doch* ist sie nur eine Chimaire. Es scheint mir freilich zu billig, allzuleicht, wenn *Claudius* über die Prioritätsstreitigkeiten zwischen Newton und Leibniz spottet; aber es ist, glaube ich, doch wahr, daß dieser Streit nur üblen Schwächen entspringt und von ÜBLEN Menschen genährt wird. *Was* hätte Newton verloren, wenn er die Originalität Leibnizs anerkannt hätte? Gar nichts! Er hätte viel gewonnen. Und doch, wie schwer ist dieses Anerkennen, das Einem, der es versucht, wie ein Eingeständnis des eigenen Unvermögens erscheint. Nur Menschen, die Dich schätzen und zugleich *lieben*, können Dir dieses Verhalten *leicht* machen.

Es handelt sich natürlich um *Neid*. Und wer ihn fühlt, müßte sich immer sagen: »Es ist ein Irrtum! Es ist ein Irrtum! —«

Im Gefolge jeder Idee, die viel kostet, kommen eine Menge billiger; darunter auch einige, die nützlich sind.

Manchmal sieht man Ideen, wie der Astronom von uns aus weit entlegenen Sternenwelten. (Oder es scheint doch so.)

Wenn ich einen *guten* Satz geschrieben hätte, und durch Zufall wären es zwei reimende Zeilen, so wäre dies ein *Fehler*.

Aus Tolstois schlechtem Theorisieren, das Kunstwerk übertrage ›ein Gefühl‹, könnte man *viel* lernen. – Und doch könnte man es, wenn nicht den Ausdruck eines Gefühls, einen Gefühlsausdruck nennen, oder einen gefühlten Ausdruck. Und man könnte auch sagen, daß die Menschen, die ihn verstehen, gleichermaßen zu ihm ›schwingen‹, auf ihn antworten. Man könnte sagen: Das Kunstwerk will nicht *etwas anderes* übertragen, sondern sich selbst. Wie, wenn ich Einen besuche, ich nicht bloß die und die Gefühle in ihm zu erzeugen wünsche, sondern vor allem ihn besuchen, und freilich auch gut aufgenommen werden will.

Und schon erst recht unsinnig ist es, zu sagen, der Künstler wünsche, daß, was er beim Schreiben, der Andre beim Lesen fühlen solle. Ich kann wohl

value, how could anyone steal the value from me? And if the light from above is lacking, I can't in any case be more than clever.

I completely understand how someone may find it *hateful* for the priority of his invention or discovery to be disputed, and want to defend his priority 'with tooth and claw'. *All the same* this is completely chimerical. It certainly seems to me too cheap, all too easy, for *Claudius* to make fun of the squabbles between Newton and Leibniz over who was first; but it's nevertheless true, I think, that this quarrel is simply the expression of evil weaknesses and fostered by VILE people. Just *what* would Newton have lost if he had acknowledged Leibniz's originality? Absolutely nothing! He would have gained a lot. And yet, how hard it is to acknowledge something of this sort: someone who tries it feels as though he were confessing his own incapacity. Only people who hold you in esteem and at the same time *love* you can make it easy for you to behave like this.

It's a question of *envy* of course. And anyone who experiences it ought to keep on telling himself: "It's a mistake! It's a mistake! – ".

Every idea that costs a lot carries in its train a host of cheap ones; among these are even some that are useful.

Sometimes you see ideas in the way an astronomer sees stars in the far distance. (Or it seems like that anyway.)

If I were to write a *good* sentence which by accident turned out to consist of two rhyming lines, that would be a *blunder*.

There is a lot to be learned from Tolstoy's bad theorizing about how a work of art conveys 'a feeling'. – You really could call it, not exactly the expression of a feeling, but at least an expression of feeling, or a felt expression. And you could say too that in so far as people understand it, they 'resonate' in harmony with it, respond to it. You might say: the work of art does not aim to convey *something else*, just itself. Just as, when I pay someone a visit, I don't just want to make him have feelings of such and such a sort; what I mainly want is to visit him, though of course I should like to be well received too.

And it does start to get quite absurd if you say that an artist wants the feelings he had when writing to be experienced by someone else who reads his work. Presumably I can think I understand a poem (e.g.), understand it as its

glauben, ein Gedicht (z. B.) zu verstehen, es so zu verstehen, wie sein Erzeuger es sich wünschen würde, – aber was *er* beim Schreiben gefühlt haben mag, das kümmert mich *gar* nicht.

So wie ich keine Verse schreiben kann, so kann ich auch Prosa nur *soweit*, und nicht weiter, schreiben. Meiner Prosa ist eine ganz bestimmte Grenze gesetzt, und ich kann ebenso wenig über *sie* hinaus, als ich es vermöchte, ein Gedicht zu schreiben. Mein Apparat ist *so* beschaffen; nur dieser Apparat steht mir zur Verfügung. Es ist, wie wenn Einer sagte: Ich kann in diesem Spiel nur *diesen* Grad der Vollkommenheit erreichen; und nicht *jenen*.

Es ist *möglich*, daß Jeder, der eine bedeutende Arbeit leistet, eine Fortsetzung, eine Folge, seiner Arbeit im Geiste vor sich sieht, – träumt; aber es wäre doch merkwürdig, wenn es nun wirklich so käme, wie er es geträumt hat. Heute nicht an die eigenen Träume zu glauben, ist freilich leicht.

Nietzsche schreibt einmal,[1] daß auch die besten Dichter und Denker Mittelmäßiges und Schlechtes geschrieben, nur eben das Gute davon geschieden haben. Aber ganz so ist es nicht. Ein Gärtner hat in seinem Garten freilich neben den Rosen auch den Dünger und Kehricht und Stroh, aber sie unterscheiden sich nicht nur in der Güte, sondern vor allem in ihrer Funktion im Garten.

Was wie ein schlechter Satz ausschaut, kann der *Keim* zu einem guten sein.

Die Fähigkeit des ›Geschmacks‹ kann keinen Organismus schaffen, nur einen schon vorhandenen regulieren. Der Geschmack lockert Schrauben und zieht Schrauben an, er schafft nicht ein neues Uhrwerk.

Der Geschmack reguliert. Das Gebären ist nicht seine Sache.

Der Geschmack macht ANNEHMBAR.

(Darum braucht, glaube ich, der große Schöpfer keinen Geschmack; das Kind kommt wohlgeschaffen zur Welt.)

Feilen ist *manchmal* Tätigkeit des Geschmacks, manchmal nicht. *Ich* habe Geschmack.

[1] *Menschliches, Allzumenschliches*, I, § 155.

author would wish me to – but what *he* may have felt in writing it doesn't concern me *at all*.

Just as I cannot write verse, so too my ability to write prose extends only *so far*, and no farther. There is a quite definite limit to the prose I can write and I can no more overstep *that* than I can write a poem. *This* is the nature of my equipment; and it is the only equipment I have. It's as though someone were to say: In this game I can only attain *such and such* a degree of perfection, I can't go *beyond* it.

Perhaps everyone who achieves an important piece of work has an imaginative idea – a dream – of how it might be further developed; but it would all the same be remarkable if things were really to turn out according to his dream. Nowadays of course it's easy not to believe in your own dreams.

Nietzsche writes somewhere[1] that even the best poets and thinkers have written stuff that is mediocre and bad, but have separated off the good material. But it is not quite like that. It's true that a gardener, along with his roses, keeps manure and rubbish and straw in his garden, but what distinguishes them is not just their value, but mainly their function in the garden.
    Something that looks like a bad sentence can be the *germ* of a good one.

The faculty of 'taste' cannot create a new structure, it can only make adjustments to one that already exists. Taste loosens and tightens screws, it does not build a new piece of machinery.

Taste makes adjustments. Giving birth is not its affair.

Taste makes things ACCEPTABLE.

(For this reason I believe that a great creator has no need of taste; his child is born into the world fully formed.)

Sometimes polishing is a function of taste, but sometimes not. *I* have taste.

----

[1] *Human, All Too Human*, I, § 155.

Auch der *feinste* Geschmack hat mit Schöpferkraft *nichts* zu tun.

Geschmack ist Feinheit der Empfindung; Empfindung aber *tut* nicht, sie nimmt nur auf.

Ich vermag *nicht* zu beurteilen, ob ich nur Geschmack, oder auch Originalität habe. Jenen sehe ich klar, diese nicht, oder ganz undeutlich. Und vielleicht muß es so sein, und man sieht nur, was man *hat*, nicht was man ist. Wenn Einer nicht lügt, ist er originell genug. Denn die Originalität, die wünschenswert wäre, kann doch nicht eine Art Kunststück sein, oder eine Eigenheit, wie immer ausgeprägt.

Ja schon das ist ein Anfang guter Originalität, nicht sein zu wollen, was man nicht ist. Und alles das ist von Andern schon *viel* besser gesagt worden.

Geschmack kann entzücken, aber nicht ergreifen.

Man kann einen alten Stil gleichsam in einer neueren Sprache wiedergeben; ihn sozusagen neu aufführen in einem Tempo, das unsrer Zeit gemäß ist. Man ist dann eigentlich nur reproduktiv. Das habe ich beim Bauen getan.
   Was ich meine, ist aber *nicht* ein neues Zurechtstutzen eines alten Stils. Man nimmt nicht die alten Formen und richtet sie dem neuen Geschmack entsprechend her. Sondern man spricht, vielleicht unbewußt, in Wirklichkeit die alte Sprache, spricht sie aber in einer Art und Weise, die der neuern Welt, darum aber nicht notwendigerweise ihrem Geschmacke, angehört.

Der Mensch reagiert *so:* er sagt »*Nicht* das!« – und kämpft es an. Daraus entstehen vielleicht Zustände, die ebenso unerträglich sind; und vielleicht ist dann die Kraft zu weiterer Revolte verausgabt. Man sagt »Hätte *der* nicht *das* getan, so wäre das Übel nicht gekommen«. Aber mit welchem Recht? Wer kennt die Gesetze, nach denen die Gesellschaft sich entwickelt? Ich bin überzeugt, daß auch der Gescheiteste keine Ahnung hat. Kämpfst Du, so kämpfst Du. Hoffst Du, so hoffst Du.
   Man kann kämpfen, hoffen und auch glauben, ohne *wissenschaftlich* zu glauben.

Die Wissenschaft: Bereicherung und Verarmung. Die *eine* Methode drängt alle andern beiseite. Mit dieser verglichen scheinen sie alle ärmlich, höchstens

Even the *most refined* taste has *nothing* to do with creative power.

Taste is refinement of sensitivity; but sensitivity does not *do* anything, it is purely receptive.

I am *not* able to judge whether taste is all I have, or whether I have originality too. The former I can see quite clearly but not the other, or only quite indistinctly. And perhaps this is how it has to be, and you can only see what you *have*, not what you are. Someone who does not lie is already original enough. Because, after all, any originality worth wishing for could not be a sort of clever trick, or a personal peculiarity, be it as distinctive as you like.

In fact the beginnings of good originality are already there if you do not want to be something you are not. And all this has been said before *much* better by other people.

Taste can be charming, but not gripping.

An old style can be translated, as it were, into a newer language; it can, one might say, be performed afresh at a tempo appropriate to our own times. To do this is really only to reproduce. That is what my building work amounted to.
   But what I mean is *not* giving an old style a fresh trim. You don't take the old forms and fix them up to suit the latest taste. No, you are really speaking the old language, perhaps without realizing it, but you are speaking it in a way that is appropriate to the modern world, without on that account necessarily being in accordance with its taste.

A man reacts *like this*: he says "No, I *won't* tolerate that!" – and resists it. Perhaps this brings about an equally intolerable situation and perhaps by then strength for any further revolt is exhausted. People say: "If *he* hadn't done *that*, the evil would have been avoided." But what justifies this? Who knows the laws according to which society develops? I am quite sure they are a closed book even to the cleverest of men. If you fight, you fight. If you hope, you hope.
   You can fight, hope and even believe without believing *scientifically*.

Science: enrichment and impoverishment. *One* particular method elbows all the others aside. They all seem paltry by comparison, preliminary stages at best.

Vorstufen. Du mußt zu den Quellen niedersteigen, um sie alle nebeneinander zu sehen, die vernachläßigtcn und die bevorzugten.

Kann *ich* nur keine Schule gründen, oder kann es ein Philosoph nie? Ich kann keine Schule gründen, weil ich eigentlich nicht nachgeahmt werden will. Jedenfalls nicht von denen, die Artikel in philosophischen Zeitschriften veröffentlichen.

Der Gebrauch des Wortes »Schicksal«. Unser Verhalten zur Zukunft und Vergangenheit. Wieweit halten wir uns für die Zukunft verantwortlich? Wieviel spekulieren wir über die Zukunft? Wie denken wir über Vergangenheit und Zukunft? Wenn etwas Unangenehmes geschieht: – fragen wir »Wer ist schuld?«, sagen wir »Jemand muß dran schuld sein«, – oder sagen wir »Es war Gottes Wille«, »Es war Schicksal«?
   Wie, eine Frage stellen, auf ihre Antwort dringen, oder sie nicht stellen, ein anderes Verhalten, eine andere Art des Lebens ausdrückt, *so*, in diesem Sinne, auch ein Ausspruch wie »Es ist Gottes Wille« oder »Wir sind nicht Herren über unser Schicksal«. Was dieser Satz tut, oder doch Ähnliches, könnte auch ein Gebot tun! Auch eins, was man sich selbst gibt. Und umgekehrt kann ein Gebot, z. B. »Murre nicht!« als Feststellung einer Wahrheit ausgesprochen werden.

Das Schicksal steht im Gegensatz zum Naturgesetz. Das Naturgesetz will man ergründen, und verwenden, das Schicksal nicht.

Es ist mir durchaus nicht klar, daß ich eine Fortsetzung meiner Arbeit durch Andre mehr wünsche, als eine Veränderung der Lebensweise, die alle diese Fragen überflüssig macht. (Darum könnte ich nie eine Schule gründen.)

Der Philosoph sagt »Sieh' die Dinge *so* an!« – aber damit ist erstens nicht gesagt, daß die Leute sie so ansehen werden, zweitens mag er überhaupt mit seiner Mahnung zu spät kommen, und es ist auch möglich, daß so eine Mahnung überhaupt nichts ausrichten kann und der Impuls zu dieser Änderung der Anschauung von anders wo kommen muß. So ist es ganz unklar, ob Bacon irgend etwas bewegt hat, außer die Oberfläche der Gemüter seiner Leser.

You must go right down to the original sources so as to see them all side by side, both the neglected and the preferred.

Am *I* the only one who cannot found a school or can a philosopher never do this? I cannot found a school because I do not really want to be imitated. Not at any rate by those who publish articles in philosophical journals.

The use of the word "fate". Our attitude to the future and the past. To what extent do we hold ourselves responsible for the future? How much do we speculate about the future? How do we think about the past and the future? If something unwelcome happens: – do we ask "Whose fault is it?", do we say "It must be somebody's fault", – or do we say "It was God's will", "It was fate"?

In the sense in which asking a question and insisting on an answer is expressive of a different attitude, a different mode of life, from not asking it, the *same* can be said of utterances like "It is God's will" or "We are not masters of our fate". The work done by this sentence, or at any rate something like it, could also be done by a command! Including one which you give yourself. And conversely the utterance of a command, such as "Don't be resentful", may be like the affirmation of a truth.

Fate is the antithesis of natural law. A natural law is something you try to fathom and make use of, but not fate.

I am by no means sure that I should prefer a continuation of my work by others to a change in the way people live which would make all these questions superfluous. (For this reason I could never found a school.)

A philosopher says "Look at things like this!" – but in the first place that doesn't ensure that people will look at things like that, and in the second place his admonition may come altogether too late; it's possible, moreover, that such an admonition can achieve nothing in any case and that the impetus for such a change in the way things are perceived has to originate somewhere else entirely. For instance it is by no means clear whether Bacon started anything moving, other than the surface of his readers' minds.

Nichts kommt mir weniger wahrscheinlich vor, als daß ein Wissenschaftler, oder Mathematiker, der mich liest, dadurch in seiner Arbeitsweise ernstlich beeinflußt werden sollte. (In sofern sind meine Betrachtungen wie die Plakate an den Kartenschaltern der englischen Bahnhöfe[1] »Is your journey really necessary?« Als ob Einer, der das liest, sich sagen würde »On second thoughts, *no*«.) Hier muß man mit ganz anderen Geschützen kommen, als ich im Stande bin, in's Feld zu führen. Am ehesten könnte ich noch dadurch eine Wirkung erzielen, daß, vor allem, durch meine Anregung eine *große* Menge Dreck geschrieben wird, und daß *vielleicht* dieser die Anregung zu etwas Gutem wird. Ich dürfte immer nur auf die aller indirekteste Wirkung hoffen.

Z. B. nichts dümmer, als das Geschwätz über Ursache und Wirkung in Büchern über Geschichte; nichts verkehrter, weniger durchdacht. – Aber wer könnte dem Einhalt tun, dadurch, daß er das *sagte*? (Es wäre, als wollte ich durch reden die Kleidung der Frauen und der Männer ändern.)

Denke dran, wie man von Labors Spiel gesagt hat »Er *spricht*«. Wie eigentümlich! Was war es, was einen in diesem Spiel so an ein Sprechen gemahnt hat? Und wie merkwürdig, daß die Ähnlichkeit mit dem Sprechen nicht etwas uns Nebensächliches, sondern etwas Wichtiges und Großes ist! – Die Musik, und gewiß *manche* Musik, möchten wir eine Sprache nennen; *manche* Musik aber gewiß nicht. (Nicht, daß damit ein Werturteil gefällt sein muß!)

Das Buch ist voller Leben – nicht wie ein Mensch, sondern wie ein Ameishaufen.

Man vergißt immer wieder, auf den Grund zu gehen. Man setzt die Fragezeichen nicht *tief* genug.

Die Wehen bei der Geburt neuer Begriffe.

»Die Weisheit ist grau.« Das Leben aber und die Religion sind farbenreich.

---

[1] Während des zweiten Weltkriegs und unmittelbar nachher.

Nothing seems to me less likely than that a scientist or mathematician who reads me should be seriously influenced in the way he works. (In that respect my reflections are like the notices on the ticket offices at English railway stations[1] "Is your journey really necessary?". As though someone who read this would think "On second thoughts *no*".) What is needed here is artillery of a completely different kind from anything I am in a position to muster. The most I might expect to achieve by way of effect is that I should first stimulate the writing of a *whole lot* of garbage and that then this *perhaps* might provoke somebody to write something good. I ought never to hope for more than the most indirect influence.

E.g. there is nothing more stupid than the chatter about cause and effect in history books; nothing is more wrong-headed, more half-baked. – But what hope could anyone have of putting a stop to it just by *saying* that? (It would be like my trying to change the way women and men dress by talking.)

Remember how it was said of Labor's playing: "He is *speaking*." How curious! What was it about this playing that was so strongly reminiscent of speech? And how remarkable that we do not find the similarity with speech incidental, but something important, big! – Music, *some* music at least, makes us want to call it a language; but some music of course doesn't. (Not that this need involve any judgement of value!)

The book is full of life – not like a man, but like an ant-heap.

One keeps forgetting to go right down to the foundations. One doesn't put the question marks *deep* enough down.

The labour pains at the birth of new concepts.

"Wisdom is grey." Life on the other hand and religion are full of colour.

---

[1] During and immediately after the Second World War.

Es könnte sein, daß die Wissenschaft und Industrie, und ihr Fortschritt, das Bleibendste der heutigen Welt ist. Daß jede Mutmaßung eines Zusammenbruchs der Wissenschaft und Industrie einstweilen, und auf *lange* Zeit, ein bloßer Traum sei, und daß Wissenschaft und Industrie nach und mit unendlichem Jammer die Welt einigen werden, ich meine, sie zu *einem* zusammenfassen werden, in welchem dann freilich alles eher als der Friede wohnen wird.

Denn die Wissenschaft und die Industrie entscheiden doch die Kriege, oder so scheint es.

Interessiere Dich nicht für das, was, vermeintlich, Du allein faßt!

Der Kreis meiner Gedanken ist wahrscheinlich viel enger, als ich ahne.

Die Gedanken steigen, langsam, wie Blasen an die Oberfläche. (Manchmal ist es, als sähe man einen Gedanken, eine Idee, als undeutlicher Punkt fern am Horizont; und dann kommt er oft mit überraschender Geschwindigkeit näher.)

Wo schlechte Wirtschaft im Staat ist, wird, glaube ich, auch schlechte Wirtschaft in den Familien begünstigt. Der jederzeit zum Streike bereite Arbeiter wird auch seine Kinder nicht zur Ordnung erziehen.

Möge Gott dem Philosophen Einsicht geben in das, was vor allen Augen liegt.

Das Leben ist wie ein Weg auf einer Bergschneide; rechts und links glitscherige Abhänge, auf denen Du in dieser, oder jener Richtung unaufhaltsam hinunterrutschst. Immer wieder sehe ich Menschen so rutschen und sage »Wie könnte sich ein Mensch da helfen!« Und *das* heißt: »den freien Willen leugnen«. Das ist die Stellungnahme, die sich in diesem ›Glauben‹ ausdrückt. Er ist aber kein *wissenschaftlicher* Glaube, hat nichts mit wissenschaftlichen Überzeugungen zu tun.

Die Verantwortung *leugnen*, heißt, den Menschen nicht zur Verantwortung *ziehen*.

Science and industry, and their progress, might turn out to be the most enduring thing in the modern world. Perhaps any speculation about a coming collapse of science and industry is, for the present and for a *long* time to come, nothing but a dream; perhaps science and industry, having caused infinite misery in the process, will unite the world – I mean condense it into a *single* unit, though one in which peace is the last thing that will find a home.

Because science and industry do decide wars, or so it seems.

Don't concern yourself with what, presumably, no one but you grasps!

My thoughts probably move in a far narrower circle than I suspect.

Thoughts rise to the surface slowly, like bubbles. (Sometimes it's as though you could see a thought, an idea, as an indistinct point far away on the horizon; and then it often approaches with astonishing swiftness.)

I believe that bad housekeeping within the state fosters bad housekeeping in families. A workman who is constantly ready to go on strike will not bring up his children to respect order either.

God grant the philosopher insight into what lies in front of everyone's eyes.

Life is like a path along a mountain ridge; to left and right are slippery slopes down which you slide without being able to stop yourself, in one direction or the other. I keep seeing people slip like this and I say "How could a man help himself in such a situation!". And *that* is what "denying free will" comes to. That is the attitude expressed in this 'belief'. But it is not a *scientific* belief and has nothing to do with scientific convictions.

Denying responsibility is not *holding* people responsible.

Manche Menschen haben einen Geschmack, der sich zu einem ausgebildeten verhält, wie der Gesichtseindruck eines halb blinden Auges zu dem eines normalen. Wo das normale Auge klare Artikulation sieht, sieht das schwache verwaschene Farbflecke.

Wer zu viel weiß, für den ist es schwer nicht zu lügen.

Ich habe eine solche Angst davor, daß jemand im Hause Klavier spielt, daß ich, wenn es geschehen ist und das Klimpern aufgehört hat, noch eine Art Halluzination habe, als ginge es weiter. Ich kann es dann ganz deutlich hören, obwohl ich weiß, daß es nur in meiner Einbildung ist.

Es kommt mir vor, als könne ein religiöser Glaube nur etwas wie das leidenschaftliche Sich-entscheiden für ein Bezugssystem sein. Also obgleich es *Glaube* ist, doch eine Art des Lebens, oder eine Art das Leben zu beurteilen. Ein leidenschaftliches Ergreifen *dieser* Auffassung. Und die Instruktion in einem religiösen Glauben müßte also die Darstellung, Beschreibung jenes Bezugssystems sein und zugleich ein in's-Gewissen-reden. Und diese beiden müßten am Schluß bewirken, daß der Instruierte selber, aus eigenem, jenes Bezugssystem leidenschaftlich erfaßt. Es wäre, als ließe mich jemand auf der einen Seite meine hoffnungslose Lage sehen, auf der andern stellte er mir das Rettungswerkzeug dar, bis ich, aus eigenem, oder doch jedenfalls nicht von dem *Instruktor* an der Hand geführt, auf das zustürzte und es ergriffe.

Einmal wird vielleicht aus dieser Zivilisation eine Kultur entspringen.
    Dann wird es eine wirkliche Geschichte der Erfindungen des 18., 19. und 20. Jahrhunderts geben, die voll von tiefem Interesse sein wird.

Wir sagen in einer wissenschaftlichen Untersuchung alles mögliche; machen viele Aussagen, deren Rolle in der Untersuchung wir nicht verstehen. Denn wir sagen ja nicht etwa alles mit einem bewußten Zweck, sondern unser Mund geht eben. Wir gehen durch herkömmliche Gedankenbewegungen, machen, automatisch, Gedankenübergänge gemäß den Techniken, die wir gelernt haben. Und nun müssen wir erst, was wir gesagt haben, sichten. Wir haben eine ganze Menge unnütze, ja zweckwidrige Bewegungen gemacht, müssen nun unsere Gedankenbewegungen philosophisch klären.

Some people's taste is to an educated taste as is the visual impression received by a purblind eye to that of a normal eye. Where a normal eye will see something clearly articulated, a weak eye will see a blurred patch of colour.

Someone who knows too much finds it hard not to lie.

I am so afraid of someone's playing the piano in the house that, when this happens and then the tinkling stops, I have a sort of hallucination of its still going on. I can hear it quite clearly even though I know that it's all in my imagination.

It strikes me that a religious belief could only be something like a passionate commitment to a system of reference. Hence, although it's *belief*, it's really a way of living, or a way of assessing life. It's passionately seizing hold of *this* interpretation. Instruction in a religious faith, therefore, would have to take the form of a portrayal, a description, of that system of reference, while at the same time being an appeal to conscience. And this combination would have to result in the pupil himself, of his own accord, passionately taking hold of the system of reference. It would be as though someone were first to let me see the hopelessness of my situation and then show me the means of rescue until, of my own accord, or not at any rate led to it by my *instructor*, I ran to it and grasped it.

Perhaps one day this civilization will produce a culture.
    When that happens there will be a real history of the discoveries of the 18th, 19th and 20th Centuries, which will be deeply interesting.

In the course of a scientific investigation we say all kinds of things; we make many utterances whose role in the investigation we do not understand. For it isn't as though everything we say has a conscious purpose; our tongues just keep going. Our thoughts run in established routines, we pass automatically from one thought to another according to the techniques we have learned. And now comes the time for us to survey what we have said. We have made a whole lot of movements that do not further our purpose, or that even impede it, and now we have to clarify our thought processes philosophically.

Mir scheint, ich bin noch weit von dem Verständnis dieser Dinge, nämlich von dem Punkt, wo ich weiß, worüber ich sprechen muß, und worüber ich nicht zu sprechen brauche. Ich verwickle mich immer noch in Einzelheiten, ohne zu wissen, ob ich über diese Dinge überhaupt reden sollte; und es kommt mir vor, daß ich vielleicht ein großes Gebiet begehe, nur um es einmal aus der Betrachtung auszuschließen. Auch in diesem Falle aber wären diese Betrachtungen nicht wertlos; wenn sie sich nämlich nicht etwa nur im Kreise herumbewegen.

1948

Beim Philosophieren muß man in's alte Chaos hinabsteigen, und sich dort wohlfühlen.

Genie ist das Talent, worin der Charakter sich ausspricht. Darum, möchte ich sagen, hatte Kraus Talent, ein außerordentliches Talent, aber nicht Genie. Es gibt freilich Genieblitze, bei denen man dann, trotz des *großen* Talenteinsatzes, das Talent nicht merkt. Beispiel: »Denn tun können auch die Ochsen und die Esel . . .«.[1] Es ist merkwürdig, daß das z. B. so viel größer ist, als irgend etwas, was Kraus je geschrieben hat. Es ist hier eben nicht ein Verstandesskelett, sondern ein ganzer Mensch.

Das ist auch der Grund, warum die Größe dessen, was Einer schreibt, von allem Übrigen abhängt, was er schreibt und tut.

Im Traum, und auch *lange* nach dem Erwachen, können uns Traumworte die höchste Bedeutung zu haben scheinen. Ist nicht die gleiche Illusion auch im Wachen möglich? Es kommt mir so vor, als unterläge *ich* ihr jetzt manchmal. Bei Verrückten scheint es oft so.

Was ich hier schreibe, mag schwächliches Zeug sein; nun dann bin ich nicht im Stande, das Große, Wichtige herauszubringen. Aber es liegen in diesen schwächlichen Bemerkungen große Ausblicke verborgen.

Schiller schreibt in einem Brief (ich glaube an Goethe)[2] von einer »poetischen Stimmung«. Ich glaube, ich weiß, was er meint, ich glaube sie selbst zu

---

[1] Lichtenberg, *Timorus*, Vorrede. Vollständig lautet der Satz: »Denn tun können auch die Ochsen und die Esel, aber versichern kann noch zur Zeit der Mensch nur allein.«
[2] Brief an Goethe, 17. December 1795.

It seems to me I am still a long way from understanding these things, a long way from the point of knowing what I do and what I don't need to discuss. I still keep getting entangled in details without knowing whether I ought to be talking about such things at all; and I have the impression that I may be inspecting a large area only eventually to exclude it from consideration. But even in that case these reflections wouldn't be worthless; as long, that is, as they are not just going round in a circle.

1948

When you are philosophizing you have to descend into primeval chaos and feel at home there.

Genius is talent in which character makes itself heard. That is why I want to say that Kraus had talent, an exceptional talent, but not genius. There are certainly flashes of genius such that despite the *great* infusion of talent, you do not notice the talent. An example: "For the ox and the ass can do things too...".[1] It is remarkable how much greater that is than anything Kraus, e.g., ever wrote. This is no mere intellectual skeleton, but a complete human being.

That too is why the greatness of what a man writes depends on everything else he writes and does.

During a dream and even *long* after we have woken up, words occurring in the dream can strike us as having the greatest significance. Can't we be subject to the same illusion when awake? I have the impression that *I* am sometimes liable to this nowadays. The insane often seem to be like this.

What I am writing here may be feeble stuff; well, then I am just not capable of bringing the big, important thing to light. But hidden in these feeble remarks are great prospects.

In a letter (to Goethe I think)[2] Schiller writes of a "poetic mood". I think I know what he means, I believe I am familiar with it myself. It is a mood of

---

[1] Georg Christoph Lichtenberg, *Timorus*, Preface. The complete sentence reads: "For the ox and the ass can do things too, but up to now only a man can give you an assurance."

[2] Letter to Goethe, 17th December 1795.

kennen. Es ist die Stimmung, in welcher man für die Natur empfänglich ist und in welcher die Gedanken so lebhaft erscheinen, wie die Natur. Merkwürdig ist aber, daß Schiller nicht besseres hervorgebracht hat (oder so scheint es mir) und ich bin daher auch gar nicht sicher überzeugt, daß, was *ich* in solcher Stimmung hervorbringe, wirklich etwas Wert ist. Es ist wohl möglich, daß meine Gedanken ihren Glanz dann nur von einem Licht, das *hinter* ihnen steht, empfangen. Daß sie nicht *selbst* leuchten.

Wo Andre weitergehn, dort bleib ich stehn.

[Zum Vorwort.][1] Nicht ohne Widerstreben übergebe ich das Buch zur Öffentlichkeit. Die Hände, in die es geraten wird, sind zumeist nicht diejenigen, in denen ich es mir gerne vorstelle. Möge es – das wünsche ich ihm – bald gänzlich von den philosophischen Journalisten vergessen werden, und so vielleicht einer bessern Art von Lesern aufbewahrt bleiben.

Von den Sätzen, die ich hier niederschreibe, macht immer nur jeder so und so vielte einen Fortschritt; die andern sind wie das Klappen der Schere des Haarschneiders, der sie in Bewegung erhalten muß, um mit ihr im rechten Moment einen Schnitt zu machen.

Sowie ich auf entlegeneren Gebieten fortwährend Fragen antreffe, die ich nicht beantworten kann, wird es verständlich, warum ich mich in weniger entlegenen noch nicht auskenne. Denn wie weiß ich, daß, was hier die Antwort aufhält, nicht eben das ist, was dort mich hindert, den Nebel zu zerstreuen?

Rosinen mögen das Beste an einem Kuchen sein; aber ein Sack Rosinen ist nicht besser als ein Kuchen; und wer im Stande ist, uns einen Sack voll Rosinen zu geben, kann damit noch keinen Kuchen backen, geschweige, daß er etwas besseres kann. Ich denke an Kraus und seine Aphorismen, aber auch an mich selbst und meine philosophischen Bemerkungen.

Ein Kuchen, das ist nicht gleichsam: verdünnte Rosinen.

Farben regen zum Philosophieren an. Vielleicht erklärt das die Leidenschaft Goethes für die Farbenlehre.

[1] Für *Philosophische Untersuchungen*.

receptivity to nature in which one's thoughts seem as vivid as nature itself. But it is strange that Schiller did not produce anything better (or so it seems to me) and so I am not entirely convinced that what *I* produce in such a mood is really worth anything. It may be that what gives my thoughts their lustre on these occasions is a light shining on them from behind. That they do not *themselves* glow.

Where others go on ahead, I stay in one place.

(For the Preface.)[1] It is not without reluctance that I deliver this book to the public. It will fall into hands which are not for the most part those in which I like to imagine it. May it soon – this is what I wish for it – be completely forgotten by the philosophical journalists, and so be preserved perhaps for a better sort of reader.

  Only every now and again does one of the sentences that I write here make a step forward; the rest are like the snipping of the barber's scissors, which he has to keep moving so as to make a cut with them at the right moment.

As long as I continue to come across questions in more remote regions which I can't answer, it is understandable that I should still not be able to find my way around regions that are less remote. For how do I know that what stands in the way of an answer here is not precisely what is preventing me from clearing away the fog over there?

Raisins may be the best part of a cake; but a bag of raisins is not better than a cake; and someone who is in a position to give us a bag full of raisins still can't bake a cake with them, let alone do something better. I am thinking of Kraus and his aphorisms, but of myself too and my philosophical remarks.

  A cake – that isn't as it were: thinned-out raisins.

Colours spur us to philosophize. Perhaps that explains Goethe's passion for the theory of colours.

---

[1] For *Philosophical Investigations*.

Die Farben scheinen uns ein Rätsel aufzugeben, ein Rätsel, das uns anregt – nicht aufregt.

Der Mensch kann alles Schlechte in sich als Verblendung ansehen.

Wenn es wahr ist, wie ich glaube, daß Mahlers Musik nichts wert ist, dann ist die Frage, was er, meines Erachtens, mit seinem Talent hätte tun sollen. Denn ganz offenbar gehörten doch *eine Reihe sehr seltener Talente* dazu, diese schlechte Musik zu machen. Hätte er z. B. seine Symphonien schreiben und verbrennen sollen? Oder hätte er sich Gewalt antun, und sie nicht schreiben sollen? Hätte er sie schreiben, und einsehen sollen, daß sie nichts wert seien? Aber wie hätte er das einsehen können? Ich sehe es, weil ich seine Musik mit der der großen Komponisten vergleichen kann. Aber *er* konnte das nicht; denn, wem das eingefallen ist, der mag wohl gegen den Wert des Produkts *mißtrauisch* sein, weil er ja wohl sieht, daß er nicht, sozusagen, die Natur der andern großen Komponisten habe, – aber die Wertlosigkeit wird er deswegen nicht einsehen; denn er kann sich immer sagen, daß er zwar *anders* ist, als die übrigen (die er aber bewundert), aber in einer andern Art wertvoll. Man könnte vielleicht sagen: Wenn Keiner, den Du bewunderst, so ist wie Du, dann glaubst Du wohl nur darum an Deinen Wert, weil *Du's* bist. – Sogar wer gegen die Eitelkeit kämpft, aber darin nicht ganz erfolgreich ist, wird sich immer über den Wert seines Produkts täuschen.

Am gefährlichsten aber scheint es zu sein, wenn man seine Arbeit irgendwie in die Stellung bringt, wo sie, zuerst von einem selbst und dann von Andern mit den alten großen Werken verglichen wird. An solchen Vergleich sollte man gar nicht denken. Denn wenn die Umstände heute wirklich so anders sind, als die frühern, daß man sein Werk der *Art* nach nicht mit den früheren Werken vergleichen kann, dann kann man auch den *Wert* nicht mit dem eines andern vergleichen. Ich selbst mache immer wieder den Fehler, von dem hier die Rede ist.

Konglomerat: Nationalgefühl, z. B.

Tiere kommen auf den Zuruf ihres Namens. Ganz wie Menschen.

Ich frage unzählige irrelevante Fragen. Möge ich durch diesen Wald mich durchschlagen können!

Colours seem to present us with a riddle, a riddle that stimulates[1] us – not one that disturbs[1] us.

Man can regard all the evil within himself as delusion.

If it is true that Mahler's music is worthless, as I believe to be the case, then the question is what I think he ought to have done with his talent. For quite obviously it took a *set of very rare talents* to produce this bad music. Should he, say, have written his symphonies and then burnt them? Or should he have done violence to himself and not written them? Should he have written them and realized that they were worthless? But how could he have realized that? I can see it, because I can compare his music with what the great composers wrote. But *he* could not, because though perhaps someone to whom such a comparison has occurred may have *misgivings* about the value of his work through seeing, as it were, that his nature is not that of the other great composers, – that still does not mean that he will recognize its worthlessness; because he can always tell himself that though he is certainly *different* from the rest (whom he nevertheless admires), his work has a different kind of value. Perhaps we might say: If nobody you admire is like you, then presumably you believe in your own value only because you are *you*. – Even someone who is struggling against vanity will, if his struggle is not entirely successful, still deceive himself about the value of his own work.

But the greatest danger seems to lie in putting one's own work, in one way or another, into the position of being compared, first by oneself then by others, with the great works of former times. One ought to put such a comparison right out of one's mind. For if conditions nowadays are really so different from what they once were that one cannot even compare the *genre* one's work belongs to with that of earlier works, then one can't compare them in respect of their value either. I myself continually make the mistake I'm referring to.

Conglomeration: national sentiment for instance.

Animals come when their names are called. Just like human beings.

I ask countless irrelevant questions. If only I can succeed in hacking my way through this forest!

---

[1] In the German there is a play on the two cognate verbs *anregt* and *aufregt* which I have not been able to catch. (Tr.)

Ich möchte eigentlich durch meine häufigen Interpunktionszeichen das Tempo des Lesens verzögern. Denn ich möchte langsam gelesen werden. (Wie ich selbst lese.)

Ich glaube, Bacon ist in seiner Philosophie stecken geblieben, und diese Gefahr droht auch mir. Er hatte eine lebhafte Vorstellung eines riesigen Gebäudes, sie entschwand ihm aber doch, wenn er wirklich in's Einzelne gehen wollte. Es war, als hätten Menschen seiner Zeit begonnen, ein großes Gebäude von den Fundamenten aufzuführen; und als hätte er in der Phantasie so etwas Ähnliches, die Erscheinung solches Gebäudes, gesehen, sie noch stolzer gesehen, als die vielleicht, die am Bau arbeiteten. Dazu war eine *Ahnung* der Methode nötig, aber durchaus nicht Talent zum Bauen. Das Schlimme aber war, daß er polemisch gegen die eigentlichen Bauleute vorging und *seine* Grenzen entweder nicht kannte, oder nicht erkennen wollte.

Anderseits ist es aber ungeheuer schwierig diese Grenzen zu sehen, und d. h., klar darzustellen. Also, sozusagen, eine Malweise aufzufinden, dieses Unklare darzustellen. Denn ich möchte mir immer sagen: »Mal wirklich nur, was Du siehst!«

Der Traum wird bei der Freudschen Analyse sozusagen zersetzt. Er verliert seinen ersten Sinn *völlig*. Man könnte sich denken, daß er auf dem Theater gespielt würde, daß die Handlung des Stücks manchmal etwas unverständlich, aber zum Teil auch ganz verständlich wäre, oder doch uns schiene, und als würde nun diese Handlung in kleine Teile zerrissen und jedem Teil ein gänzlich andrer Sinn gegeben. Man könnte es sich auch so denken: Es wird auf ein großes Blatt Papier ein Bild gezeichnet und das Blatt nun solcher Art gefältelt, daß im ersten Bild ganz unzusammenhörige Stücke fürs Auge aneinander stoßen und ein neues, sinnvolles oder sinnloses, Bild entsteht (dies wäre der geträumte Traum, das erste Bild der ›latente Traumgedanke‹).

Ich könnte mir nun denken, daß Einer, der das entfaltete Bild sieht, ausriefe »Ja, das ist die Lösung, das ist, was ich geträumt habe, aber ohne Lücken und Entstellungen«. Es wäre dann eben diese Anerkennung, die die Lösung zur Lösung machte. Sowie, wenn Du beim Schreiben ein Wort suchst und nun sagst: »*Das* ist es, *das* sagt, was ich wollte!« – Deine Anerkennung das Wort zum gefundenen, also gesuchten stempelt. (Hier könnte man wirklich sagen: erst wenn man gefunden hat, wisse man, was man gesucht hat – ähnlich wie Russell über das Wünschen redet.)

Was am Traum intriguiert, ist nicht sein *kausaler* Zusammenhang mit Geschehnissen meines Lebens, etc., sondern eher dies, daß er wie ein Teil einer Geschichte wirkt, und zwar ein sehr *lebendiger*, wovon der Rest im Dunkeln liegt. (Man möchte fragen: »Woher kam diese Gestalt nun, und was ist aus ihr geworden?«) Ja, auch wenn mir Einer nun zeigt, daß diese Geschichte gar

I really want my copious punctuation marks to slow down the speed of reading. Because I should like to be read slowly. (As I myself read.)

I believe Bacon got bogged down in his philosophical work, and this is a danger that threatens me too. He had a vivid image of a huge building which, however, faded when he really wanted to get down to details. It was as though his contemporaries had begun to erect a great building, from the foundations up; and as though he, in his imagination, had seen something similar, a vision of such a building, an even more imposing vision perhaps than that of those doing the building work. For this he needed to have an *inkling* of the method of construction, but no talent whatever for building. But the bad thing about it was that he launched polemical attacks on the real builders and did not recognize his *own* limitations, or else did not want to.

But it is, on the other hand, enormously difficult to discern these limitations, i.e. to depict them clearly. Or, as one might say, to invent a style of painting capable of depicting what is, in this way, fuzzy. For I want to keep telling myself: "Make sure you really do paint only what you see!"

In Freudian analysis a dream is dismantled, as it were. It loses its original sense *completely*. We might think of it as of a play enacted on the stage, with a plot that's pretty incomprehensible at times, but at times too quite intelligible, or apparently so; we might then suppose this plot torn into little fragments and each of these given a completely new sense. Or we might think of it in the following way: a picture is drawn on a big sheet of paper which is then so folded that pieces which don't belong together at all in the original picture now appear side by side to form a new picture, which may or may not make sense. (This latter would correspond to the manifest dream, the original picture to the 'latent dream thought'.)

Now I could imagine that someone seeing the unfolded picture might exclaim "Yes, that's the solution, that's what I dreamed, minus the gaps and distortions". This would then be the solution precisely by virtue of his acknowledging it as such. It's like searching for a word when you are writing and then saying: "*That's* it, *that* expresses what I intended!" – Your acceptance certifies the word as having been found and hence as being the one you were looking for. (In this instance we could really say: we don't know what we are looking for until we have found it – which is like what Russell says about wishing.)

What is intriguing about a dream is not its *causal* connection with events in my life, etc., but rather the impression it gives of being a fragment of a story – a very *vivid* fragment to be sure – the rest of which remains obscure. (We feel like asking: "where did this figure come from then and what became of it?")

keine richtige Geschichte war; daß in Wirklichkeit eine ganz andere ihr zugrunde lag, so daß ich enttäuscht ausrufen möchte »Ach, *so war es?*«, so ist hier doch scheinbar etwas gestohlen worden. Freilich, die erste Geschichte zerfällt nun, wie sich das Papier auseinanderfaltet; der Mann, den ich sah, war von *da* genommen, seine Worte von *dort*, die Umgebung im Traume wieder von wo anders; aber die Traumgeschichte hat dennoch ihren eigenen Reiz, wie ein Gemälde, das uns anzieht und inspiriert.

Man kann nun freilich sagen, daß wir das Traumbild inspiriert *betrachten*, daß wir eben inspiriert *sind*. Denn, wenn wir einem Andern unsern Traum erzählen, so inspiriert ihn das Bild meistens nicht. Der Traum berührt uns wie eine entwicklungsschwangere Idee.

Circa 1947–1948

Architektur verewigt und verherrlicht etwas. Darum kann es Architektur nicht geben, wo nichts zu verherrlichen ist.[1]

1948

Schlage Geld aus jedem Fehler.

Das Verstehen und die Erklärung einer musikalischen Phrase. – Die einfachste Erklärung ist manchmal eine Geste; eine andere wäre etwa ein Tanzschritt, oder Worte, die einen Tanz beschreiben. – Aber ist denn nicht das Verstehen der Phrase ein Erlebnis, während wir sie hören? Und was tut nun die Erklärung? Sollen wir an sie denken, während wir die Musik hören? Sollen wir uns den Tanz, oder was immer es ist, dabei vorstellen? Und wenn wir's tun, – warum soll man *das* ein verständnisvolles Hören der Musik nennen?? Kommt's auf's Sehen des Tanzes an, so wäre es ja besser, *er* würde vorgeführt, statt der Musik. Alles das aber ist ein *Miß*verständnis.

Ich gebe Einem eine Erklärung, sage ihm »Es ist wie wenn . . .«; nun sagt er »Ja, jetzt verstehe ich's« oder »Ja, jetzt weiß ich, wie es zu spielen ist«. Vor allem mußte er ja die Erklärung nicht *annehmen;* es ist ja nicht, als hätte ich ihm sozusagen überzeugende Gründe dafür gegeben, daß diese Stelle vergleichbar ist dem und dem. Ich erkläre ihm ja, z. B., nicht ⟨aus⟩[2] Äußerungen des Komponisten, diese Stelle habe das und das darzustellen.

Wenn ich nun frage »Was erlebe ich denn eigentlich, wenn ich dies Thema höre und mit Verständnis höre?« – so kommen mir nichts als Plattheiten in den

---

[1] Mehrere Varianten im Manuskript.   [2] Textstelle unklar.

What's more, if someone now shows me that this story is not the right one; that in reality it was based on quite a different story, so that I want to exclaim disappointedly "Oh, *that*'s how it was?", it really is as though I have been deprived of something. The original story certainly disintegrates now, as the paper is unfolded; the man I saw was taken from over *here*, his words from over *there*, the surroundings in the dream from somewhere else again; but all the same the dream story has a charm of its own, like a painting that attracts and inspires us.

It can certainly be said that contemplation of the dream-image inspires us, that we just *are* inspired. Because if we tell someone else our dream the image will not usually inspire him. The dream affects us as does an idea pregnant with possible developments.

Circa 1947–1948

Architecture immortalizes and glorifies something. Hence there can be no architecture where there is nothing to glorify.[1]

1948

Strike a coin from every mistake.

Understanding and explaining a musical phrase. – Sometimes the simplest explanation is a gesture; on another occasion it might be a dance step, or words describing a dance. – But isn't understanding the phrase experiencing something whilst we hear it? In that case what part does the explanation play? Are we supposed to think of it as we hear the music? Are we supposed to imagine the dance, or whatever it may be, while we listen? And suppose we do do this – why should *that* be called listening to the music with understanding? If seeing the dance is what is important, it would be better to perform *that* rather than the music. But that is all *mis*understanding.

I give someone an explanation and tell him "It's as though . . ."; then he says "Yes, now I understand it" or "Yes, now I see how it's to be played." It's most important that he didn't have to *accept* the explanation; it's not as though I had, as it were, given him conclusive reasons for thinking that this passage should be compared with that and the other one. I don't, e.g., explain to him that according[2] to things the composer has said this passage is supposed to represent such and such.

If I now ask "So what do I actually experience when I hear this theme and

---

[1] Several variations in the manuscript.   [2] Text unclear.

Kopf zur Antwort. So etwas wie Vorstellungen, Bewegungsempfindungen, Erinnerungen u. dergl.

Ich sage freilich »Ich gehe mit« – aber was heißt das? Es *könnte* so etwas heißen wie: ich begleite die Musik mit Gebärden. Und wenn man darauf hinweist, daß das doch meistens nur in sehr rudimentärem Maße vor sich geht, erhält man etwa die Antwort, die rudimentären Bewegungen werden durch Vorstellungen ergänzt. Aber nehmen wir doch an, es begleite Einer die Musik in vollem Maße durch Bewegungen, – inwiefern ist *das* ihr Verständnis? Und will ich sagen, die Bewegungen seien das Verstehen; oder seine Bewegungsempfindungen? (Was weiß ich von denen?) – Wahr ist, daß ich seine Bewegungen, unter Umständen, als Zeichen seines Verständnisses ansehen werde.

Soll ich aber (wenn ich Vorstellungen, Bewegungsempfindungen, etc. als Erklärung zurückweise) sagen, es sei eben das Verstehen ein spezifisches, nicht weiter analysierbares Erlebnis? Nun, das ginge an, wenn es nicht heißen soll: es sei ein spezifischer *Erlebnisinhalt*. Denn bei *diesen* Worten denkt man eigentlich an Unterschiede wie die zwischen Sehen, Hören und Riechen.

Wie erklärt man denn Einem, was es heißt »Musik verstehen«? Indem man ihm die Vorstellungen, Bewegungsempfindungen, etc. nennt, die der Verstehende hat? *Eher noch*, indem man ihm die Ausdrucksbewegungen des Verstehenden zeigt. – Ja, die Frage ist auch, welche Funktion hat das Erklären hier? Und was heißt es: verstehen, was es heißt, Musik zu verstehen? Mancher würde ja sagen: das zu verstehen heiße: selbst Musik zu verstehen. Und die Frage wäre also »Kann man Einen denn lehren, Musik zu verstehen?«, denn nur so ein Unterricht wäre eine Erklärung der Musik zu nennen.

Das Verständnis der Musik hat einen gewissen *Ausdruck*, sowohl während des Hörens und Spielens, als auch zu andern Zeiten. Zu diesem Ausdruck gehören manchmal Bewegungen, manchmal aber nur, wie der Verstehende das Stück spielt, oder summt, auch hier und da Vergleiche, die er zieht, und Vorstellungen, die die Musik gleichsam illustrieren. Wer Musik versteht, wird anders (mit anderem Gesichtsausdruck, z. B.) zuhören, reden, als der es nicht versteht. Sein Verständnis eines Themas wird sich aber nicht nur in Phänomenen zeigen, die das Hören oder Spielen dieses Themas begleiten, sondern in einem Verständnis für Musik im allgemeinen.

Das Verständnis der Musik ist eine Lebensäußerung des Menschen. Wie wäre sie Einem zu beschreiben? Nun, vor allem müßte man wohl die *Musik* beschreiben. Dann könnte man beschreiben, wie sich Menschen zu ihr verhalten. Aber ist das alles, was dazu nötig ist, oder gehört dazu, daß wir ihm selbst Verständnis beibringen? Nun, ihm Verständnis beibringen wird ihm in *anderem* Sinne lehren, was Verständnis ist, als eine Erklärung, die dies nicht tut. Ja auch, ihm Verständnis für Gedichte oder Malerei beibringen, kann zur Erklärung dessen gehören, was Verständnis für Musik sei.

understand what I hear?" – nothing occurs to me by way of reply except trivialities. Images, sensations of movement, recollections and such like.

Perhaps I say, "I respond to it" – but what does that mean? It might mean something like: I gesture in time with the music. And if we point out that for the most part this only happens to a very rudimentary extent, we shall probably get the reply that such rudimentary movements are filled out by images. But suppose we assume all the same that someone accompanies the music with movements in full measure, – to what extent does *that* amount to understanding it? Do I want to say that the movements he makes constitute his understanding; or his kinaesthetic sensations? (How much do I know about these?) – What is true is that in some circumstances I will take the movements he makes as a sign that he understands.

But (if I reject images, kinaesthetic sensations, etc. as an explanation), should I say that understanding is simply a specific experience that cannot be analysed any further? Well, that would be tolerable as long as it were not supposed to mean: it is a specific *experiential content*. For in point of fact *these* words make us think of distinctions like those between seeing, hearing and smelling.

So how do we explain to someone what "understanding music" means? By specifying the images, kinaesthetic sensations, etc., experienced by someone who understands? *More likely*, by drawing attention to his expressive movements. – And we really ought to ask what function explanation has here. And what it means to speak of: understanding what it means to understand music. For some would say: to understand that means: to understand music itself. And in that case we should have to ask "Well, can someone be taught to understand music?", for that is the only sort of teaching that could be called explaining music.

There is a certain *expression* proper to the appreciation of music, in listening, playing, and at other times too. Sometimes gestures form part of this expression, but sometimes it will just be a matter of how a man plays, or hums, the piece, now and again of the comparisons he draws and the images with which he as it were illustrates the music. Someone who understands music will listen differently (e.g. with a different expression on his face), he will talk differently, from someone who does not. But he will show that he understands a particular theme not just in manifestations that accompany his hearing or playing that theme but in his understanding for music in general.

Appreciating music is a manifestation of the life of mankind. How should we describe it to someone? Well, I suppose we should first have to describe *music*. Then we could describe how human beings react to it. But is that all we need do, or must we also teach him to understand it for himself? Well, getting him to understand and giving him an explanation that does not achieve this will be "teaching him what understanding is" in *different* senses of that phrase. And again, teaching him to understand poetry or painting may contribute to teaching him what is involved in understanding music.

Unsre Kinder lernen schon in der Schule, Wasser *bestehe* aus den Gasen Wasserstoff und Sauerstoff, oder Zucker aus Kohlenstoff, Wasserstoff und Sauerstoff. Wer es nicht versteht ist dumm. Die wichtigsten Fragen werden zugedeckt.

Die Schönheit einer Sternfigur – eines Sechseck-Sterns etwa – wird beeinträchtigt, wenn man sie symmetrisch bezüglich einer bestimmten Achse sieht.

Bach hat gesagt, er habe alles nur durch Fleiß geleistet. Aber ein solcher Fleiß setzt eben Demut und eine ungeheure Leidensfähigkeit, also Kraft, voraus. Und wer sich dann vollkommen ausdrücken kann, spricht eben zu uns die Sprache eines großen Menschen.

Ich glaube, daß die Erziehung der Menschen heute dahingeht, die Leidens-fähigkeit zu verringern. Eine Schule gilt heute für gut, ›if the children have a good time‹. Und das war früher *nicht* der Maßstab. Und die Eltern möchten, daß die Kinder werden, wie sie selbst sind (only more so) und doch lassen sie sie durch eine Erziehung gehen, die von der ihren *ganz* verschieden ist. – Auf die Leidensfähigkeit gibt man nichts, denn Leiden soll es nicht geben, sie sind eigentlich veraltet.

»Die Tücke des Objekts.« – Ein unnötiger Anthropomorphismus. Man könnte von einer Tücke der *Welt* reden; sich leicht vorstellen, der Teufel habe die Welt geschaffen, oder einen Teil von ihr. Und es ist *nicht* nötig, ein Eingreifen des Dämons von Fall zu Fall sich vorzustellen; es kann alles ›den Naturgesetzen entsprechend‹ vor sich gehen; es ist dann eben der ganze Plan von vornherein auf's Schlimme angelegt. Der Mensch aber befindet sich in dieser Welt, in der die Dinge zerbrechen, rutschen, alles mögliche Unheil anstiften. Und er ist natürlich eins von den Dingen. – Die ›Tücke‹ des Objekts ist ein dummer Anthropomorphismus. Denn die Wahrheit ist viel ernster als diese Fiktion.

Ein stilistischer Behelf mag praktisch sein, und mir doch verboten. Das Schopenhauer'sche »als welcher« z. B. Es würde den Ausdruck manchmal bequemer, deutlicher, machen, kann aber nicht von dem gebraucht werden, der es als altväterisch empfindet; und er darf sich nicht über diese Empfindung hinwegsetzen.

While still at school our children get taught that water *consists* of the gases hydrogen and oxygen, or sugar of carbon, hydrogen and oxygen. Anyone who doesn't understand is stupid. The most important questions are concealed.

The beauty of a star-shaped figure – a hexagonal star, say – is impaired if we regard it as symmetrical relatively to a given axis.

Bach said that all his achievements were simply the fruit of industry. But industry like that requires humility and an enormous capacity for suffering, hence strength. And someone who, with all this, can also express himself perfectly, simply speaks to us in the language of a great man.

I think the way people are educated nowadays tends to diminish their capacity for suffering. At present a school is reckoned good 'if the children have a good time'. And that used *not* to be the criterion. Parents moreover want their children to grow up like themselves (only more so), but nevertheless subject them to an education *quite* different from their own. – Endurance of suffering isn't rated highly because there is supposed not to be any suffering – really it's out of date.

"The cussedness of things." – An unnecessary anthropomorphism. We might speak of the *world* as malicious; we could easily imagine the Devil had created the world, or part of it. And it is *not* necessary to imagine the evil spirit intervening in particular situations; everything can happen 'according to the laws of nature'; it is just that the whole scheme of things will be aimed at evil from the very start. But man exists in this world, where things break, slide about, cause every imaginable mischief. And of course he is one such thing himself. – The 'cussedness' of things is a stupid anthropomorphism. Because the truth is much graver than this fiction.

A stylistic device may be useful and yet I may be barred from using it. Schopenhauer's "as which" for instance. Sometimes this would make for much more comfortable and clearer expression, but if someone feels it is archaic, he cannot use it; and he must not disregard this feeling either.

Religiöser Glaube und Aberglaube sind ganz verschieden. Der eine entspringt aus *Furcht* und ist eine Art falscher Wissenschaft. Der andre ist ein Vertraun.

Es wäre beinahe seltsam, wenn es nicht Tiere mit dem Seelenleben von Pflanzen gäbe. D. h., mit dem mangelnden Seelenleben.

Als ein Grundgesetz der Naturgeschichte könnte man es, glaube ich, betrachten, daß, wo immer etwas in der Natur ›eine Funktion hat‹, ›einen Zweck erfüllt‹, dieses selbe auch vorkommt, wo es keinen erfüllt, ja ›unzweckdienlich‹ ist.

Erhalten die Träume manchmal den Schlaf, so kannst Du darauf rechnen, daß sie ihn manchmal stören; erfüllt die Traumhalluzination manchmal einen *plausiblen* Zweck (der eingebildeten Wunscherfüllung), so rechne darauf, daß sie auch das Gegenteil tut. Eine ›dynamische Theorie der Träume‹[1] gibt es nicht.

Worin liegt die Wichtigkeit des genauen Ausmalens von Anomalien? Kann man es nicht, so zeigt das, daß man sich in den Begriffen nicht auskennt.

Ich bin zu weich, zu schwach, und darum zu faul, um Bedeutendes zu leisten. Der Fleiß der Großen ist, unter andrem, ein Zeichen ihrer *Kraft*, abgesehen auch von ihrem inneren Reichtum.

Wenn Gott wirklich die zu errettenden Menschen *wählt*, dann ist kein Grund, warum er sie nicht nach Nationen, Rassen, oder Temperamenten wählen soll. Warum die Wahl nicht in den Naturgesetzen ihren Ausdruck haben soll. (Er *konnte* ja auch so wählen, daß die Wahl einem Gesetz folgt.)

Ich habe Auszüge aus den Schriften von St. John of the Cross[2] gelesen, Leute seien zu Grunde gegangen, weil sie nicht das Glück hatten, im richtigen Moment einen weisen geistlichen Führer zu finden.

Und wie kann man dann sagen, Gott versuche den Menschen nicht über seine Kräfte?

Ich bin hier zwar geneigt, zu sagen, daß schiefe Begriffe viel Unheil angerichtet haben, aber die Wahrheit ist, daß ich gar *nicht weiß*, was Heil und was Unheil anstiftet.

---

[1] Freud.
[2] Des hl. Johannes vom Kreuz.

Religious faith and superstition are quite different. One of them results from *fear* and is a sort of false science. The other is a trusting.

It would almost be strange if there did not exist animals with the mental life of plants. I.e. lacking mental life.

I think it might be regarded as a basic law of natural history that wherever something in nature 'has a function', 'serves a purpose', the same thing can also be found in circumstances where it serves no purpose and is even 'dysfunctional'.

If dreams sometimes protect sleep, you can count on their sometimes disturbing it; if dream hallucination sometimes serves a *plausible* purpose (of imaginary wish fulfilment), count on its doing the opposite as well. There is no 'dynamic theory of dreams'.[1]

What is important about depicting anomalies precisely? If you cannot do it, that shows you do not know your way around the concepts.

I am too soft, too weak, and so too lazy to achieve anything significant. The industry of great men is, amongst other things, a sign of their *strength*, quite apart from their inner wealth.

If God really does choose those who are to be saved, there is no reason why he should not choose them according to nationality, race or temperament. Or why the choice should not find expression in the laws of nature. (Certainly he was *able* so to choose that his choice should follow a law.)

I have read excerpts from the writings of St. John of the Cross where he says that people have fallen into the pit because they did not have the good fortune to find a wise spiritual director at the right moment.

And if that is so, how can anyone say that God does not try men beyond their strength?

What I really feel like saying here is that distorted concepts have done a lot of mischief, but the truth is that I just *do not know* what does good and what does mischief.

[1] Freud.

Wir dürfen nicht vergessen: auch unsere feineren, mehr philosophischen Bedenken haben eine instinktive Grundlage. Z. B. das ›Man‹ kann nie wissen .... Das Zugänglichbleiben für weitere Argumente. Leute, denen man das nicht beibringen könnte, kämen uns geistig minderwertig vor. *Noch* unfähig einen gewissen Begriff zu bilden.

Wenn Nachtträume eine ähnliche Funktion haben, wie Tagträume, so dienen sie zum Teil dazu, den Menschen auf *jede* Möglichkeit (auch die schlimmste) vorbereiten.

Wenn Einer mit voller Sicherheit an Gott glauben kann, warum dann nicht an der Andern Seele?

Diese musikalische Phrase ist für mich eine Gebärde. Sie schleicht sich in mein Leben ein. Ich mache sie mir zu eigen.
    Die unendlichen Variationen des Lebens sind unserm Leben wesentlich. Und also eben der Gepflogenheit des Lebens. Ausdruck *besteht* für uns ⟨in⟩[1] Unberechenbarkeit. Wüßte ich genau, wie er sein Gesicht verziehen, sich bewegen wird, so wäre kein Gesichtausdruck, keine Gebärde vorhanden. – Stimmt das aber? – Ich kann mir doch ein Musikstück, das ich (ganz) auswendig weiß, immer wieder anhören; und es könnte auch von einer Spieluhr gespielt werden. Seine Gebärden blieben für mich immer Gebärden, obgleich ich immer weiß, was kommen wird. Ja, ich kann sogar immer wieder überrascht sein. (In einem bestimmten Sinne.)

Der ehrliche religiöse Denker ist wie ein Seiltänzer. Er geht, dem Anscheine nach, beinahe nur auf der Luft. Sein Boden ist der schmalste, der sich denken läßt. Und doch läßt sich auf ihm wirklich gehen.

Der feste Glaube. (An eine Verheißung z. B.) Ist er weniger sicher als die Überzeugung von einer mathematischen Wahrheit? – Aber werden dadurch die Sprachspiele ähnlicher!

---

[1] Vermutung d. Herausgebers.

We must not forget: even our more refined, more philosophical doubts have a foundation in instinct. E.g. that expressed in 'We can never know . . .'. Continuing accessibility to further arguments. We should find people to whom we could not teach this mentally inferior. *Still* incapable of forming a certain concept.

If the dreams we have in sleep have a similar function to day dreams, part of their purpose is to prepare a man for *any* eventuality (including the worst).

If someone can believe in God with complete certainty, why not in Other Minds?

For me this musical phrase is a gesture. It insinuates itself into my life. I adopt it as my own.

Life's infinite variations are essential to our life. And so too even to the habitual character of life. What we regard as expression *consists* in incalculability. If I knew exactly how he would grimace, move, there would be no facial expression, no gesture. – Is that true though? – I can after all listen again and again to a piece of music that I know (completely) by heart; and it might even be played on a musical box. Its gestures would still be gestures for me, even though I knew all the time what was going to come next. Indeed, I might even keep being surprised. (In a certain sense.)

An honest religious thinker is like a tightrope walker. He almost looks as though he were walking on nothing but air. His support is the slenderest imaginable. And yet it really is possible to walk on it.

Unshakable faith. (E.g. in a promise.) Is it any less certain than being convinced of a mathematical truth? – But does that make the language games any more alike!

Es ist für unsre Betrachtung wichtig, daß es Menschen gibt, von denen jemand fühlt, er werde nie wissen, was in ihnen vorgeht. Er werde sie nie verstehen. (Engländerinnen für Europäer.)

Ich glaube, es ist eine wichtige und merkwürdige Tatsache, daß ein musikalisches Thema, wenn es in (sehr) verschiedenen Tempi gespielt wird, seinen *Charakter* ändert. Übergang von der Quantität zur Qualität.

Die Probleme des Lebens sind an der Oberfläche unlösbar, und nur in der Tiefe zu lösen. In den Dimensionen der Oberfläche sind sie unlösbar.

In einer Konversation: Einer wirft einen Ball; der Andre weiß nicht: soll er ihn zurückwerfen, oder einem Dritten zuwerfen, oder liegenlassen, oder aufheben und in die Tasche stecken, etc.

Der große Architekt in einer schlechten Periode (Van der Nüll) hat eine ganz andere Aufgabe als der große Architekt in einer guten Periode. Man darf sich wieder nicht durch das allgemeine Begriffswort verführen lassen. Nimm nicht die Vergleichbarkeit, sondern die Unvergleichbarkeit als selbstverständlich hin.

Nichts ist doch wichtiger, als die Bildung von fiktiven Begriffen, die uns die unseren erst verstehen lehren.

»Denken ist schwer« (Ward). Was heißt das eigentlich? Warum ist es schwer? – Es ist beinahe ähnlich, als sagte man »Schauen ist schwer«. Denn angestrengtes Schauen ist schwer. Und man kann angestrengt schauen und doch nichts sehen, oder immer wieder etwas zu sehen glauben, und doch nicht deutlich sehen können. Man kann müde werden vom Schauen, auch wenn man nichts sieht.

Wenn Du einen Knäuel nicht entwirren kannst, so ist das Gescheiteste, was Du tun kannst, das einzusehen; und das Anständigste, es zuzugestehen. [Antisemitismus.]
        Was man tun soll, das Übel zu heilen, ist *nicht* klar. Was man *nicht* tun darf, ist von Fall zu Fall klar.

It is important for our view of things that someone may feel concerning certain people that their inner life will always be a mystery to him. That he will never understand them. (Englishwomen in the eyes of Europeans.)

I think it an important and remarkable fact that a musical theme alters its *character* if it is played at (very) different tempi. A transition from quantity to quality.

The problems of life are insoluble on the surface and can only be solved in depth. They are insoluble in surface dimensions.

In a conversation: One person throws a ball; the other does not know: whether he is supposed to throw it back, or throw it to a third person, or leave it on the ground, or pick it up and put it in his pocket, etc.

In a bad period the task facing a great architect (Van der Null) is completely different from what it is in a good period. You must not let yourself be seduced by the terminology in common currency. Don't take comparability, but rather incomparability, as a matter of course.

Nothing is more important for teaching us to understand the concepts we have than constructing fictitious ones.

"Thinking is difficult" (Ward). What does this really mean? Why is it difficult? – It is almost like saying "Looking is difficult". Because looking intently is difficult. And it's possible to look intently without seeing anything, or to keep thinking you see something without being able to see clearly. Looking can tire you even when you don't see anything.

When you can't unravel a tangle, the most sensible thing is for you to recognize this; and the most honourable thing, to admit it. [Antisemitism.]
    What you ought to do to remedy the evil is *not* clear. What you must *not* do is clear in particular cases.

Es ist merkwürdig, daß man die Zeichnungen von Busch oft ›metaphysisch‹ nennen kann. So gibt es also eine Zeichenweise, die metaphysisch ist? – »Gesehen mit dem Ewigen als Hintergrund«[1] könnte man sagen. Aber doch bedeuten diese Striche das nur in einer ganzen Sprache. Und es ist eine Sprache ohne Grammatik, man könnte ihre Regeln nicht angeben.

Karl der Große hat im Alter vergebens versucht, schreiben zu lernen: und so kann Einer auch vergebens trachten, eine Gedankenbewegung zu erlernen. Sie wird ihm nie geläufig.

Eine Sprache, in der im Takt geredet wird, so daß man auch nach dem *Metronom* reden kann. Es ist nicht selbstverständlich, daß Musik sich, wie die unsere, wenigstens beiläufig, metronomieren läßt. (Das Thema aus der 8. Symphonie[2] genau nach dem Metronom zu spielen.)

Schon in Menschen, die sämtlich die gleichen Gesichtszüge hätten, könnten wir uns nicht finden.

Ist ein falscher Gedanke nur einmal kühn und klar ausgedrückt, so ist damit schon viel gewonnen.

Nur wenn man noch viel verrückter denkt, als die Philosophen, kann man ihre Probleme lösen.

Denk, jemand sähe ein Pendel an und dächte dabei: So läßt Gott es gehen. Hat denn Gott nicht die Freiheit, auch einmal in Übereinstimmung mit einer Rechnung zu handeln?

Ein weit talentierterer Schriftsteller als ich hätte noch immer geringes Talent.

Es ist ein *körperliches* Bedürfnis des Menschen, sich bei der Arbeit zu sagen »Jetzt lassen wir's schon einmal«, und daß man immer wieder gegen dieses

---

[1] Vgl. *Tagebücher*, 7. 10. 1916.
[2] Achte Symphonie Beethovens.

It is queer that Busch's drawings can often be called 'metaphysical'. Is there such a thing as a metaphysical style of drawing then? – "Seen against the background of the eternal",[1] you might say. However, these strokes have such a meaning only within a whole language. And it is a language without grammar; you couldn't say what its rules are.

When he was old Charlemagne tried to learn to write, but without success: and similarly someone may fail when he tries to acquire a manner of thinking. He never becomes fluent in it.

A language which is spoken in strict tempo and which can, therefore, also be spoken in time with a *metronome*. It isn't a matter of course that music should be performable as ours is, at least optionally, to the metronome. (Playing the theme from the 8th Symphony[2] exactly in time with the metronome.)

Suppose we were to meet people who all had the same facial features: that would be enough for us not to know where we were with them.

Even to have expressed a false thought boldly and clearly is already to have gained a great deal.

It's only by thinking even more crazily than philosophers do that you can solve their problems.

Imagine someone watching a pendulum and thinking: God makes it move like that. Well, isn't God equally free to act in accordance with a calculation?

A writer far more talented than I would still have only a minor talent.

To say, when they are at work, "Let's have done with it now", is a *physical* need for human beings; it is the constant necessity when you are

---

[1] Cf. *Notebooks*, 7.10.1916.
[2] Beethoven's Eighth Symphony.

Bedürfnis beim Philosophieren denken muß, macht diese Arbeit so anstrengend.

Du mußt die Fehler Deines eigenen Stiles *hinnehmen*. Beinahe wie die Unschönheiten des eigenen Gesichts.

Steige immer von den kahlen Höhen der Gescheitheit in die grünenden Täler der Dummheit.

Ich habe eines von diesen Talenten, das immer wieder aus der Not eine Tugend machen muß.

Tradition ist nichts, was Einer lernen kann, ist nicht ein Faden, den Einer aufnehmen kann, wenn es ihm gefällt; so wenig, wie es möglich ist, sich die eigenen Ahnen auszusuchen.
  Wer eine Tradition nicht hat und sie haben möchte, der ist wie ein unglücklich Verliebter.

Der glücklich Verliebte und der unglücklich Verliebte haben Jeder sein eigenes Pathos.
  Aber es ist schwerer gut unglücklich verliebt sein, als gut glücklich verliebt.

Moore hat mit seinem Paradox in ein philosophisches Wespennest gestochen; und wenn die Wespen nicht gehörig aufgeflogen sind, so ist es nur, weil sie zu träg waren.

Im Geistigen läßt sich ein Unternehmen meistens nicht fortsetzen, soll auch gar nicht fortgesetzt werden. Diese Gedanken düngen den Boden für eine neue Saat.

So bist Du also ein schlechter Philosoph, wenn, was Du schreibst, schwer verständlich ist? Wärest Du besser, so würdest Du das Schwere leicht verständlich machen. – Aber wer sagt, daß das möglich ist?! [Tolstoi.]

philosophizing to go on thinking in the face of this need that makes this such strenuous work.

You have to accept the faults in your own style. Almost like the blemishes in your own face.

Never stay up on the barren heights of cleverness, but come down into the green valleys of silliness.

I have one of those talents that constantly has to make a virtue out of necessity.

Tradition is not something a man can learn; not a thread he can pick up when he feels like it; any more than a man can choose his own ancestors.
    Someone lacking a tradition who would like to have one is like a man unhappily in love.

There is a pathos peculiar to the man who is happily in love as well as to the one who is unhappily in love.
    But it is harder to bear yourself well when you are unhappily in love than when you are happily in love.

Moore stirred up a philosophical wasps' nest with his paradox; and the only reason the wasps did not duly fly out was that they were too listless.

In the sphere of the mind someone's project cannot usually be continued by anyone else, nor should it be. These thoughts will fertilize the soil for a new sowing.

Are you a bad philosopher then, if what you write is hard to understand? If you were better you would make what is difficult easy to understand. – But who says that's possible?! [Tolstoy].

Das größte Glück des Menschen ist die Liebe. Angenommen, Du sagst vom Schizophrenischen: er liebt nicht, er kann nicht lieben, er will nicht lieben – wo ist der Unterschied?!

»Er will nicht . . .« heißt: es ist in seiner Macht. Und *wer* will das sagen?!
   Wovon sagt man denn »es ist in meiner Macht«? – Man sagt es, wo man einen Unterschied machen will. *Dies* Gewicht kann ich heben, will's aber nicht heben; jenes *kann* ich nicht heben.

»Gott hat es befohlen, also muß man's tun können.« Das heißt gar nichts. Hier ist kein ›*also*‹. Die beiden Ausdrücke könnten höchstens das *gleiche* bedeuten.
   »Er hat es befohlen« heißt hier ungefähr: Er wird strafen, wer es nicht tut. Und daraus folgt nichts über das Können. Und *das* ist der Sinn der ›Gnadenwahl‹.
   Das heißt aber nicht, daß es richtig ist, zu sagen: »Er straft, obgleich man nicht anders *kann*.« – Wohl aber könnte man sagen: Hier wird gestraft, wo der Mensch nicht strafen dürfte. Und der Begriff der ›Strafe‹ überhaupt ändert sich hier. Denn die alten Illustrationen lassen sich hier nicht mehr anwenden, oder müssen nun ganz anders angewendet werden. Sieh Dir nur eine Allegorie an, wie »The Pilgrim's Progress«, und wie hier alles – im menschlichen Sinne – nicht stimmt. – Aber stimmt sie nicht doch? D. h.: läßt sie sich nicht anwenden? Sie ist ja angewendet worden. (Auf den Bahnhöfen gibt es Zifferblätter mit zwei Zeigern; sie zeigen an, wann der nächste Zug abfährt. Sie schauen aus wie Uhren und sind keine; haben aber ihre Verwendung.) (Es gäbe hier ein besseres Gleichnis.)
   Dem Menschen, der bei dieser Allegorie unwillig wird, könnte man sagen: Verwende sie anders oder kümmere Dich nicht um sie! (Aber *manchen* wird sie weit mehr verwirren, als sie ihm helfen kann.)

Was der Leser auch kann, das überlaß dem Leser.

Ich schreibe beinahe immer Selbstgespräche mit mir selbst. Sachen, die ich mir unter vier Augen sage.

Ehrgeiz ist der Tod des Denkens.

Man's greatest happiness is love. Suppose you say of the schizophrenic: he does not love, he cannot love, he refuses to love – what is the difference?!

"He refuses to . . ." means: it is in his power. And *who* wants to say that?!

Well, what kind of thing do we say "is in my power"? – We may say this when we want to draw a distinction. I can lift *this* weight, but I am not going to do it; I *cannot* lift that one.

"God has commanded it, therefore it must be possible to do it." That means nothing. There is no '*therefore*' about it. At most the two expressions might mean the *same*.

In this context "He has commanded it" means roughly: He will punish anybody who doesn't do it. And nothing follows from that about what anybody can or cannot do. And *that* is what 'predestination' means.

But that doesn't mean that it's right to say: "He punishes you even though you *cannot* do otherwise." – Perhaps, though, one might say: in this case punishment is inflicted in circumstances where it would be impermissible for men to inflict it. And then the whole concept of 'punishment' changes. For now you can no longer use the old illustrations, or else you have to apply them quite differently. Just look at an allegory like "The Pilgrim's Progress" and notice how nothing is right – in human terms. – But isn't it right all the same? I.e.: can't it be applied? Indeed, it has been applied. (On railway stations there are dials with two hands; they show when the next train leaves. They look like clocks though they aren't; but they have a use of their own.) (It ought to be possible to find a better simile.)

If anyone gets upset by this allegory, one might say to him: Apply it differently, or else leave it alone! (But there are *some* whom it will confuse far more than it can help.)

Anything your reader can do for himself leave to him.

Nearly all my writings are private conversations with myself. Things that I say to myself tête-à-tête.

Ambition is the death of thought.

Humor ist keine Stimmung, sondern eine Weltanschauung. Und darum, wenn es richtig ist, zu sagen, im Nazi-Deutschland sei der Humor vertilgt worden, so heißt das nicht so etwas wie, man sei nicht guter Laune gewesen, sondern etwas viel Tieferes und Wichtigeres.

Zwei Menschen, die zusammen, über einen Witz etwa, lachen. Einer hat gewisse etwas ungewöhnliche Worte gebraucht und nun brechen sie beide in eine Art von Meckern aus. Das könnte Einem, der aus anderer Umgebung zu uns kommt, *sehr* sonderbar vorkommen. Während wir es ganz *vernünftig* finden.

(Ich beobachtete diese Szene neulich in einem Omnibus und konnte mich in Einen hineindenken, der das nicht gewohnt ist. Es kam mir dann ganz irrational vor und wie die Reaktionen eines uns fremden *Tiers*.)

1949

Der Begriff des ›Festes‹. Für uns mit Lustbarkeit verbunden; zu einer andern Zeit möglicherweise nur mit Furcht und Grauen. Was wir »Witz« und was wir »Humor« nennen, hat es gewiß in andern Zeiten nicht gegeben. Und diese beiden ändern sich beständig.

»Le style c'est l'homme«, »Le style c'est l'homme même«. Der erste Ausdruck hat eine billige epigrammatische Kürze. Der zweite, richtige, eröffnet eine ganz andere Perspektive. Er sagt, daß der Stil das *Bild* des Menschen sei.

Es gibt Bemerkungen, die säen, und Bemerkungen, die ernten.

Die Landschaft dieser Begriffsverhältnisse aus ihren unzähligen Stücken, wie sie die Sprache uns zeigt, zusammenstellen, ist *zu schwer* für mich. Ich kann es nur sehr unvollkommen tun.

Wenn ich mich für eine Eventualität vorbereite, kannst Du ziemlich sicher sein, daß sie nicht eintreten wird. u. U.

Es ist *schwer* etwas zu wissen, und zu handeln, als wüßte man's nicht.

Humour is not a mood but a way of looking at the world. So if it is correct to say that humour was stamped out in Nazi Germany, that does not mean that people were not in good spirits, or anything of that sort, but something much deeper and more important.

Two people are laughing together, say at a joke. One of them has used certain somewhat unusual words and now they both break out into a sort of bleating. That might appear *very* extraordinary to a visitor coming from quite a different environment. Whereas we find it completely *reasonable*.

(I recently witnessed this scene on a bus and was able to think myself into the position of someone to whom this would be unfamiliar. From that point of view it struck me as quite irrational, like the responses of an outlandish *animal*.)

1949

The concept of a 'festivity'. We connect it with merrymaking; in another age it may have been connected with fear and dread. What we call "wit" and "humour" doubtless did not exist in other ages. And both are constantly changing.

"Le style c'est l'homme", "Le style c'est l'homme même". The first expression has cheap epigrammatic brevity. The second, correct version opens up quite a different perspective. It says that a man's style is a *picture* of him.

There are remarks that sow and remarks that reap.

The relations between these concepts form a landscape which language presents us with in countless fragments; piecing them together is *too hard* for me. I can make only a very imperfect job of it.

If I prepare myself for some eventuality, you can be pretty sure that it will not happen. Given the right sort of case.

It is *difficult* to know something and to act as if you did not know it.

Es gibt wirklich die Fälle, in denen Einem der Sinn dessen, was er sagen will, viel klarer vorschwebt, als er ihn in Worten auszudrücken vermag. (Mir geschieht dies sehr oft.) Es ist dann, als sähe man deutlich ein Traumbild vor sich, könnte es aber nicht so beschreiben, daß der Andre es auch sieht. Ja, das Bild steht für den Schreiber (mich) oft bleibend hinter den Worten, so daß sie es *für mich* zu beschreiben *scheinen*.

Ein mittelmäßiger Schriftsteller muß sich hüten, einen rohen, inkorrekten Ausdruck zu schnell durch einen korrekten zu ersetzen. Dadurch tötet er den ersten Einfall, der doch noch ein lebendes Pflänzchen war. Und nun ist er dürr und *gar* nichts mehr wert. Man kann ihn nun auf den Mist werfen. Während das armselige Pflänzchen noch immer einen gewissen Nutzen hatte.

Das Veralten von Schriftstellern, die schließlich etwas *waren*, hängt damit zusammen, daß ihre Schriften von der ganzen Umgebung ihrer Zeit ergänzt, stark zu den Menschen sprechen, daß sie aber ohne diese Ergänzung sterben, gleichsam der Beleuchtung beraubt, die ihnen Farbe gab.

Und damit, glaube ich, hängt die Schönheit mathematischer Demonstrationen zusammen, wie sie selbst von Pascal empfunden wurde. In *dieser* Anschauung der Welt hatten diese Demonstrationen *Schönheit* – nicht das, was oberflächliche Menschen Schönheit nennen. Auch, ein Krystall ist nicht in jeder ›Umgebung‹ schön – obwohl vielleicht in jeder *reizvoll*. —

Wie sich ganze Zeiten nicht aus den Zangen gewisser Begriffe befreien können – des Begriffes ›schön‹ und ›Schönheit‹ z. B.

Mein eigenes Denken über Kunst und Werte ist weit desillusionierter, als es das der Menschen vor 100 Jahren sein *konnte*. Und doch heißt das nicht, daß es deswegen richtiger ist. Es heißt nur, daß im Vordergrund meines Geistes Untergänge sind, die nicht im *Vordergrund* jener waren.

Sorgen sind wie Krankheiten; man muß sie hinnehmen: das Schlimmste, was man tun kann, ist, sich gegen sie auflehnen.

Sie kommen auch in Anfällen, durch innere, oder äußere Anlässe ausgelöst. Und man muß sich dann sagen: »Wieder ein Anfall.«

Wissenschaftliche Fragen können mich interessieren, aber nie wirklich fesseln. Das tun für mich nur *begriffliche* und *ästhetische* Fragen. Die Lösung wissenschaftlicher Probleme ist mir, im Grunde, gleichgültig; jener andern Fragen aber nicht.

There really are cases where someone has the sense of what he wants to say much more clearly in his mind than he can express in words. (This happens to me very often.) It is as though one had a dream image quite clearly before one's mind's eye, but could not describe it to someone else so as to let him see it too. As a matter of fact, for the writer (myself) it is often as though the image stays there behind the words, so that they *seem* to describe it *to me*.

A mediocre writer must beware of too quickly replacing a crude, incorrect expression with a correct one. By doing so he kills his original idea, which was at least still a living seedling. Now it is withered and no longer worth *anything*. He may as well throw it on the rubbish heap. Whereas the wretched little seedling was still worth something.

One reason why authors become dated, even though they once *amounted* to something, is that their writings, when reinforced by their contemporary setting, speak strongly to men, whereas without this reinforcement their works die, as if bereft of the illumination that gave them their colour.

There is some connection between this and the beauty of mathematical demonstrations, as experienced by Pascal. Within *that* way of looking at the world these demonstrations did have *beauty* – not what superficial people call beauty. Again, a crystal is not beautiful in just any 'setting' – though perhaps it always looks *attractive*. –

Strange that whole epochs can't free themselves from the grip of certain concepts – the concept of 'beautiful' and 'beauty' for instance.

My own thinking about art and values is far more disillusioned than would have been *possible* for someone 100 years ago. That doesn't mean, though, that it's more correct on that account. It only means that I have examples of degeneration in the forefront of my mind which were not in the *forefront* of men's minds then.

Troubles are like illnesses; you have to accept them: the worst thing you can do is rebel against them.

You get attacks of them too, triggered off by internal or external causes. And then you just have to tell yourself: "Another attack."

I may find scientific questions interesting, but they never really grip me. Only *conceptual* and *aesthetic* questions do that. At bottom I am indifferent to the solution of scientific problems; but not the other sort.

Auch wenn man nicht in Kreisen denkt, so geht man doch, manchmal geradenwegs durch's Walddickicht der Fragen in's Freie hinaus, manchmal auf verschlungenen, oder Zickzackwegen, die uns nicht in's Freie führen.

Der Sabbath ist nicht einfach die Zeit der Ruhe, der Erholung. Wir sollten unsre Arbeit von außen betrachten, nicht nur von innen.

Der Gruß der Philosophen unter einander sollte sein: »Laß Dir Zeit!«

Für den Menschen ist das Ewige, Wichtige, oft durch einen undurchdringlichen Schleier verdeckt. Er weiß: da drunten ist etwas, aber er *sieht* es nicht. Der Schleier reflektiert das Tageslicht.

Warum soll der Mensch nicht todunglücklich werden? Es ist eine seiner Möglichkeiten. Wie im ›Corinthian Bagatel‹ dieser Weg der Kugel einer der möglichen Wege. Und vielleicht nicht einmal einer der seltenen.

In den Tälern der Dummheit wächst für den Philosophen noch immer mehr Gras, als auf den kahlen Höhen der Gescheitheit.

Die Zeitlichkeit der Uhr und die Zeitlichkeit in der Musik. Sie sind durchaus nicht gleiche Begriffe.
   Streng im Takt gespielt, heißt nicht genau nach dem Metronom gespielt. Es wäre aber möglich, daß eine gewisse *Art* von Musik nach dem Metronom zu spielen wäre. (Ist das Anfangsthema ⟨des zweiten Satzes⟩[1] der 8. Symphonie von dieser Art?)

Könnte man den Begriff der Höllenstrafen auch anders, als durch den Begriff der Strafe erklären? Oder den Begriff der Güte Gottes auch anders, als durch den Begriff der Güte?
   Wenn Du mit Deinen Worten die rechte *Wirkung* erzielen willst, gewiß nicht.

---

[1] Zusatz des Herausgebers.

Even when you aren't thinking in circles, you may still sometimes stride straight through the thicket of questions out into the open, and at other times wander along tortuous or zigzagging paths which don't lead out into the open at all.

The Sabbath is not simply a time for rest, for relaxation. We ought to contemplate our labours from without and not just from within.

This is how philosophers should salute each other: "Take your time!"

What is eternal and important is often hidden from a man by an impenetrable veil. He knows: there's something under there, but he cannot *see* it. The veil reflects the daylight.

Why shouldn't a man become desperately unhappy? It is one human possibility. As in 'Corinthian Bagatelle', this is one of the possible paths that the balls may take. And perhaps not even one of the unusual ones.

For a philosopher there is more grass growing down in the valleys of silliness than up on the barren heights of cleverness.

The temporality of the clock and temporality in music. They are not by any means equivalent concepts.
    Playing in *strict* tempo does not mean playing according to the metronome. Though it may be that a certain *sort* of music should be played by metronome. (Is the opening theme ⟨of the second movement⟩[1] of the 8th Symphony of this sort?)

Could you explain the concept of the punishments of hell without using the concept of punishment? Or that of God's goodness without using the concept of goodness?
    If you want to get the right *effect* with your words, certainly not.

[1] Editor's addition.

Denke, es würde Einem gelehrt: Es gibt ein Wesen, welches Dich, wenn
Du das und das tust, so und so lebst, nach Deinem Tod an einen Ort der
ewigen Qual bringen wird; die meisten Menschen kommen dorthin, eine
geringe Anzahl an einen Ort der ewigen Freude. – Jenes Wesen hat von
vornherein die ausgewählt, die an den guten Ort kommen sollen, und, da nur
die an den Ort der Qual kommen, die eine bestimmte Art des Lebens geführt
haben, die andern auch, von vornherein, zu dieser Art des Lebens bestimmt.

Wie so eine Lehre wohl wirken würde?

Es ist hier also von Strafe keine Rede, sondern eher von einer Art
Naturgesetzlichkeit. Und, wem man es in diesem Lichte darstellt, der könnte
nur Verzweiflung oder Unglauben aus dieser Lehre ziehen.

Diese Lehre könnte keine ethische Erziehung sein. Und wen man ethisch
erziehen und dennoch so lehren wollte, dem müßte man die Lehre, *nach* der
ethischen Erziehung, als eine Art unbegreiflichen Geheimnisses darstellen.

»Er hat sie, in seiner Güte, erwählt und er wird Dich strafen« hat ja keinen
Sinn. Die beiden Hälften gehören zu verschiedenen Betrachtungsarten. Die
zweite Hälfte ist ethisch und die erste ist es nicht. Und mit der ersten
zusammen ist die zweite absurd.

Der Reim von ›Rast‹ mit ›Hast‹ ist ein Zufall. Aber ein glücklicher Zufall, und
Du kannst diesen glücklichen Zufall *entdecken*.

In Beethovens Musik findet sich zum ersten Mal, was man den Ausdruck der
Ironie nennen kann. Z. B. im ersten Satz der Neunten. Und zwar ist es bei
ihm eine fürchterliche Ironie, etwa die des Schicksals. – Bei Wagner kommt
die Ironie wieder, aber in's Bürgerliche gewendet.

Man könnte wohl sagen, daß Wagner und Brahms, jeder in andrer Art,
Beethoven nachgeahmt haben; aber was bei ihm kosmisch war, wird bei
ihnen irdisch.

Es kommen bei ihm die gleichen Ausdrücke vor, aber sie folgen andern
Gesetzen.

Das Schicksal spielt ja auch in Mozarts oder Haydns Musik keinerlei Rolle.
Damit *beschäftigt* sich diese Musik nicht.

Tovey, dieser Esel, sagt einmal dies, oder etwas Ähnliches, habe damit zu
tun, daß Mozart Lektüre einer gewissen Art gar nicht zugänglich gewesen sei.
Als ob es ausgemacht wäre, daß nur die Bücher die Musik der Meister

Suppose someone were taught: there is a being who, if you do such and such or live thus and thus, will take you to a place of everlasting torment after you die; most people end up there, a few get to a place of everlasting happiness. – This being has selected in advance those who are to go to the good place and, since only those who have lived a certain sort of life go to the place of torment, he has also arranged in advance for the rest to live like that.

What might be the effect of such a doctrine?

Well, it does not mention punishment, but rather a sort of natural necessity. And if you were to present things to anyone in this light, he could only react with despair or incredulity to such a doctrine.

Teaching it could not constitute an ethical upbringing. If you wanted to bring someone up ethically while yet teaching him such a doctrine, you would have to teach it to him *after* having educated him ethically, representing it as a sort of incomprehensible mystery.

"Out of his goodness he has chosen them and he will punish you" makes no sense. The two halves of the proposition belong to different ways of looking at things. The second half is ethical, the first not. And taken together with the first, the second is absurd.

It is an accident that 'fast' rhymes with 'last'.[1] But it is a lucky accident, and you can *discover* this lucky accident.

In Beethoven's music what may be called the expression of irony makes an appearance for the first time. E.g. in the first movement of the Ninth. With him, moreover, it's a terrible irony, the irony of fate perhaps. – Irony reappears with Wagner, but this time transposed into the civic mode.

You could no doubt say that both Wagner and Brahms, each in his different way, imitated Beethoven; but what in him was cosmic becomes earthly with them.

The same expressions occur in his music, but obeying different laws. In Mozart's or Haydn's music again, fate plays no role of any sort. That is not the *concern* of this music.

That ass Tovey says somewhere that this, or something similar, is due to the fact that Mozart had no access to literature of a certain sort. As if it had been proved that the masters' music had been made what it was solely by books. Certainly, music and books are connected. But if Mozart found no great

[1] 'Rast' = 'rest'; 'Hast' = 'haste'. (Tr.)

bestimmt hätten. Freilich hängen Musik und Bücher zusammen. Aber wenn Mozart in seiner Lektüre nicht große *Tragik* fand, fand er sie darum nicht im *Leben?* Und sehen Komponisten immer nur durch die Brillen der Dichter?

Einen dreifachen Kontrapunkt gibt es nur in einer ganz bestimmten musikalischen Umgebung.

Der seelenvolle Ausdruck in der Musik. Er ist nicht nach Graden der Stärke und des Tempos zu beschreiben. Sowenig wie der seelenvolle Gesichtsausdruck durch räumliche Maße. Ja er ist auch nicht durch ein Paradigma zu erklären, denn das gleiche Stück kann auf unzählige Arten mit echtem Ausdruck gespielt werden.

Das Wesen Gottes verbürge seine Existenz – d. h. eigentlich, daß es sich hier um eine Existenz nicht handelt.

Könnte man denn nicht auch sagen, das Wesen der Farbe verbürge ihre Existenz? Im Gegensatz etwa zum weißen Elephanten. Denn es heißt ja nur: Ich kann nicht erklären, was ›Farbe‹ ist, was das Wort »Farbe« bedeutet, außer an der Hand des Farbmusters. Es gibt also hier nicht ein Erklären, ›wie es *wäre*, wenn es Farben *gäbe*‹.

Und man könnte nun sagen: Es läßt sich beschreiben, wie es wäre, wenn es Götter auf dem Olymp gäbe – aber nicht: ›wie es wäre, wenn es Gott gäbe‹. Und damit wird der Begriff ›Gott‹ näher bestimmt.

Wie wird uns das Wort »Gott« beigebracht (d. h. sein Gebrauch)? Ich kann davon keine ausführliche grammatische Beschreibung geben. Aber ich kann sozusagen Beiträge zu der Beschreibung machen; ich kann darüber manches sagen und vielleicht mit der Zeit eine Art Beispielsammlung anlegen.

Bedenke hier, daß man in einem Wörterbuch vielleicht gern solche Gebrauchsbeschreibungen gäbe, in Wirklichkeit aber nur einige wenige Beispiele und Erklärungen gibt. Ferner aber, daß mehr auch nicht nötig ist. Was könnten wir mit einer ungeheuer langen Beschreibung anfangen? – Nun, wir könnten nichts mit ihr anfangen, wenn es sich um den Gebrauch von Wörtern uns geläufiger Sprachen handelte. Aber wie, wenn wir so eine Beschreibung des Gebrauchs eines assyrischen Worts vorfänden? Und in welcher Sprache? Nun, in einer andern uns bekannten. – In der Beschreibung wird oft das Wort »manchmal« vorkommen, oder »öfters«, oder »für gewöhnlich«, oder »fast immer«, oder »fast nie«.

Es ist schwer, sich ein gutes Bild einer solchen Beschreibung zu machen.

Und ich bin im Grunde doch ein Maler, und oft ein sehr schlechter Maler.

tragedy in what he read, does that mean he did not encounter it in his *life*? And do composers never see anything except through the spectacles of poets?

Only in a quite particular musical context is there such a thing as three-part counterpoint.

Tender expression in music. It isn't to be characterized in terms of degrees of loudness or tempo. Any more than a tender facial expression can be described in terms of the distribution of matter in space. As a matter of fact it can't even be explained by reference to a paradigm, since there are countless ways in which the same piece may be played with genuine expression.

God's essence is supposed to guarantee his existence — what this really means is that what is here at issue is not the existence of something.

Couldn't one actually say equally well that the essence of colour guarantees its existence? As opposed, say, to white elephants. Because all that really means is: I cannot explain what 'colour' is, what the word "colour" means, except with the help of a colour sample. So in this case there is no such thing as explaining 'what it *would* be like if colours *were* to exist'.

And now we might say: There can be a description of what it would be like if there were gods on Olympus — but not: 'what it would be like if there were such a thing as God'. And to say this is to determine the concept 'God' more precisely.

How are we taught the word "God" (its use, that is)? I cannot give a full grammatical description of it. But I can, as it were, make some contributions to such a description; I can say a good deal about it and perhaps in time assemble a sort of collection of examples.

Remember in this connection that though we might perhaps like to give such descriptions of the use of words in a dictionary, all we in fact do is give a few examples and explanations. But remember too that no more than this is necessary. What use could we make of an enormously long description? — Well, we could do nothing with it, if it dealt with the use of words in languages that we already knew. But what if we came across such a description of the use of an Assyrian word? In what language? Let's say, in some other language already familiar to us. — The word "sometimes" will occur frequently in this description, or "often", or "usually", or "nearly always", or "almost never".

It is difficult to paint an adequate picture of what such a description might be like.

And after all a painter is basically what I am, often a very bad painter too.

Wie ist es denn, wenn Leute nicht den gleichen Sinn für Humor haben? Sie reagieren nicht richtig auf einander. Es ist, als wäre es unter gewissen Menschen Sitte einem Andern einen Ball zuzuwerfen, welcher ihn auffangen und zurückwerfen soll; aber gewisse Leute würfen ihn nicht zurück, sondern steckten ihn in die Tasche.

Oder wie ist es, wenn Einer den Geschmack des Andern gar nicht zu erraten versteht?

Ein in uns festes Bild kann man freilich dem Aberglauben vergleichen, aber doch auch sagen, daß man *immer* auf irgend einen festen Grund kommen muß, sei er nun ein Bild, oder nicht, und also sei ein Bild am Grunde alles Denkens zu respektieren und nicht als ein Aberglaube zu behandeln.

Wenn das Christentum die Wahrheit ist, dann ist alle Philosophie darüber falsch.

Kultur ist eine Ordensregel. Oder setzt doch eine Ordensregel voraus.

Die Traumerzählung, ein Gemenge von Erinnerungen. Oft zu einem sinnvollen und rätselhaften Ganzen. Gleichsam zu einem Fragment, das uns *stark* beeindruckt (*manchmal* nämlich), so daß wir nach einer Erklärung, nach Zusammenhängen suchen.

Aber warum kamen *jetzt diese* Erinnerungen? Wer will's sagen? – Es kann mit unserm gegenwärtigen Leben, also auch mit unsern Wünschen, Befürchtungen, etc., zusammenhängen. – »Aber willst Du sagen, daß diese Erscheinung im bestimmten ursächlichen Zusammenhang stehen müsse?« – Ich will sagen, daß es nicht notwendigerweise Sinn haben muß, von einem Auffinden ihrer Ursache zu reden.

Shakespeare und der Traum. Ein Traum ist ganz unrichtig, absurd, zusammengesetzt, und doch ganz richtig: er macht in *dieser* seltsamen Zusammensetzung einen Eindruck. Warum? Ich weiß es nicht. Und wenn Shakespeare groß ist, wie von ihm ausgesagt wird, dann muß man von ihm sagen können: Es ist alles falsch, *stimmt nicht* – und ist doch ganz richtig nach einem eigenen Gesetz.

Man könnte das auch so sagen: Wenn Shakespeare groß ist, kann er es nur in der *Masse* seiner Dramen sein, die sich ihre *eigene* Sprache und Welt schaffen. Er ist also ganz unrealistisch. (Wie der Traum.)

What is it like for people not to have the same sense of humour? They do not react properly to each other. It's as though there were a custom amongst certain people for one person to throw another a ball which he is supposed to catch and throw back; but some people, instead of throwing it back, put it in their pocket.

Or what is it like for somebody to be unable to fathom someone else's taste?

It is true that we can compare a picture that is firmly rooted in us to a superstition; but it is equally true that we *always* eventually have to reach some firm ground, either a picture or something else, so that a picture which is at the root of all our thinking is to be respected and not treated as a superstition.

If Christianity is the truth then all the philosophy that is written about it is false.

Culture is an observance. Or at least it presupposes an observance.

Recounting a dream, a medley of recollections. These often form a significant and enigmatic whole. They form, as it were, a fragment that makes a *powerful* impression on us (*sometimes* anyway), so that we look for an explanation, for connections.

But why did just *these* recollections occur now? Who can say? – It may be connected with our present life, and so too with our wishes, fears, etc. – "But do you want to say that this phenomenon can only exist in these particular causal surroundings?" – I want to say it does not necessarily have to make sense to speak of discovering its cause.

Shakespeare and dreams. A dream is all wrong, absurd, composite, and yet at the same time it is completely right: put together in *this* strange way it makes an impression. Why? I don't know. And if Shakespeare is great, as he is said to be, then it must be possible to say of him: it's all wrong, things *aren't like that* – and yet at the same time it's quite right according to a law of its own.

It could be put like this too: if Shakespeare is great, his greatness is displayed only in the whole *corpus* of his plays, which create their *own* language and world. In other words he is completely unrealistic. (Like a dream.)

1950

Es ist nichts Unerhörtes darin, daß der Charakter des Menschen von der Außenwelt beeinflußt werden kann (Weininger). Denn das heißt ja nur, daß erfahrungsgemäß die Menschen sich mit den Umständen ändern. Fragt man: Wie *könnte* die Umgebung den Menschen, das Ethische in ihm, *zwingen?* − so ist die Antwort, daß er zwar sagen mag »Kein Mensch muß müssen«, aber doch unter solchen Umständen so und so handeln *wird*.

›Du MUSST nicht, ich kann Dir einen (andern) Ausweg sagen, − aber Du wirst ihn nicht ergreifen.‹

Ich glaube nicht, daß man Shakespeare mit einem andern Dichter zusammen-halten kann. War er vielleicht eher ein *Sprachschöpfer* als ein Dichter?

Ich könnte Shakespeare nur anstaunen; nie etwas mit ihm anfangen.

Ich habe ein *tiefes* Mißtrauen gegen die allermeisten Bewunderer Shake-speares. Ich glaube, das Unglück ist, daß er, in der westlichen Kultur zum mindesten, einzig dasteht, und man ihn daher, um ihn einzureihen, falsch einreihen muß.

Es ist *nicht*, als ob Shakespeare Typen von Menschen gut portraitierte und insofern *wahr* wäre. Er ist *nicht* naturwahr. Aber er hat eine so gelenke Hand und einen so eigenartigen *Strich*, daß jede seiner Figuren *bedeutend*, sehenswert ausschaut.

»Das große Herz Beethovens« − niemand könnte sagen »das große Herz Shakespeares«. ›Die gelenke Hand, die neue Naturformen der Sprache geschaffen hat‹, schiene mir richtiger.

Der Dichter kann eigentlich nicht von sich sagen »Ich singe wie der Vogel singt« − aber Shakespeare hätte es vielleicht von sich sagen können.

Ein und dasselbe Thema hat in Moll einen andern Charakter als in Dur, aber von einem Charakter des Moll im allgemeinen zu sprechen, ist ganz falsch. (Bei Schubert klingt das Dur oft trauriger als das Moll.) Und so ist es, glaube ich, müßig und ohne Nutzen für das Verständnis der Malerei von den Charakteren der einzelnen Farben zu reden. Man denkt eigentlich dabei nur an spezielle Verwendungen. Daß Grün als Farbe einer Tischdecke die, Rot jene Wirkung hat, läßt auf ihre Wirkung in einem Bild keinen Schluß zu.

1950

There is nothing outrageous in saying that a man's character may be influenced by the world outside him (Weininger). Because that only means that, as we know from experience, men change with circumstances. If it is asked: How *could* a man, the ethical in a man, be *coerced* by his environment? – the answer is that even though he may say "No human being has to give way to compulsion", yet under such circumstances he *will* as a matter of fact act in such and such a way.

'You don't HAVE to, I can show you a (different) way out, – but you won't take it.'

I do not believe that Shakespeare can be set alongside any other poet. Was he perhaps a *creator of language* rather than a poet?

I could only stare in wonder at Shakespeare; never do anything with him.

I am *deeply* suspicious of most of Shakespeare's admirers. The misfortune is, I believe, that he stands by himself, at least in the culture of the west, so that one can only place him by placing him wrongly.

It is *not* as though Shakespeare portrayed human types well and were in that respect *true to life*. He is *not* true to life. But he has such a supple hand and his *brush strokes* are so individual, that each one of his characters looks *significant*, is worth looking at.

"Beethoven's great heart" – nobody could speak of "Shakespeare's great heart". 'The supple hand that created new natural linguistic forms' would seem to me nearer the mark.

A poet cannot really say of himself "I sing as the birds sing" – but perhaps Shakespeare could have said this of himself.

One and the same theme is different in character in the minor and the major, but it is quite wrong to speak generally about a character belonging to the minor key. (In Schubert the major often sounds sadder than the minor.) And similarly I think it idle and no help in understanding painting to speak of the characters of individual colours. When one speaks like that one actually only has special applications in mind. The fact that green has such and such an effect as the colour of a table cloth, red another, licenses no conclusion about their effect in a picture.

Ich glaube nicht, daß Shakespeare über das ›Dichterlos‹ hätte nachdenken können.

Er konnte sich auch nicht selbst als Prophet oder Lehrer der Menschheit betrachten.

Die Menschen staunen ihn an, beinahe wie ein Naturschauspiel. Sie fühlen nicht, daß sie dadurch mit einem großen *Menschen* in Berührung kommen. Sondern mit einem Phänomen.

Ich glaube, um einen Dichter zu genießen, dazu muß man auch die Kultur, zu der er gehört, *gern haben*. Ist die einem gleichgültig oder zuwider, so erkaltet die Bewunderung.

Wenn der an Gott Glaubende um sich sieht und fragt »Woher ist alles, was ich sehe?«, »Woher das alles?«, verlangt er *keine* (kausale) Erklärung; und der Witz seiner Frage ist, daß sie der Ausdruck dieses Verlangens ist. Er drückt also eine Einstellung zu allen Erklärungen aus. – Aber wie zeigt sich die in seinem Leben?

Es ist die Einstellung, die eine bestimmte Sache ernst nimmt, sie aber dann an einem bestimmten Punkt doch nicht ernst nimmt, und erklärt, etwas anderes sei noch ernster.

So kann Einer sagen, es ist sehr ernst, daß der und der gestorben ist, ehe er ein bestimmtes Werk vollenden konnte; und in anderem Sinne kommt's darauf gar nicht an. Hier gebraucht man die Worte »in einem tiefern Sinne«.

Eigentlich möchte ich sagen, daß es auch hier nicht auf die *Worte* ankommt, die man ausspricht, oder auf das, was man dabei denkt, sondern auf den Unterschied, den sie an verschiedenen Stellen im Leben machen. Wie weiß ich, daß zwei Menschen das gleiche meinen, wenn jeder sagt, er glaube an Gott? Und ganz dasselbe kann man bezüglich der 3 Personen sagen. Die Theologie, die auf den Gebrauch *gewisser* Worte und Phrasen dringt und andere verbannt, macht nichts klarer (Karl Barth). Sie fuchtelt sozusagen mit Worten, weil sie etwas sagen will und es nicht auszudrücken weiß. *Die Praxis* gibt den Worten ihren Sinn.

Ein Gottesbeweis sollte eigentlich etwas sein, wodurch man sich von der Existenz Gottes überzeugen kann. Aber ich denke mir, daß die *Gläubigen*, die solche Beweise lieferten, ihren ›Glauben‹ mit ihrem Verstand analysieren und begründen wollten, obgleich sie selbst durch solche Beweise nie zum Glauben gekommen wären. Einen von der ›Existenz Gottes überzeugen‹ könnte man vielleicht durch eine Art Erziehung, dadurch, daß man sein Leben so und so gestaltet.

I do not think that Shakespeare would have been able to reflect on the 'lot of the poet'.

Nor could he regard himself as a prophet or as a teacher of mankind.

People stare at him in wonderment, almost as at a spectacular natural phenomenon. They do not have the feeling that this brings them into contact with a great *human being*. Rather with a phenomenon.

I believe that if one is to enjoy a writer one has to *like* the culture he belongs to as well. If one finds it indifferent or distasteful, one's admiration cools off.

If someone who believes in God looks round and asks "Where does everything I see come from?", "Where does all this come from?", he is *not* craving for a (causal) explanation; and his question gets its point from being the expression of a certain craving. He is, namely, expressing an attitude to all explanations. – But how is this manifested in his life?

The attitude that's in question is that of taking a certain matter seriously and then, beyond a certain point, no longer regarding it as serious, but maintaining that something else is even more important.

Someone may for instance say it's a very grave matter that such and such a man should have died before he could complete a certain piece of work; and yet, in another sense, this is not what matters. At this point one uses the words "in a deeper sense".

Actually I should like to say that in this case too the *words* you utter or what you think as you utter them are not what matters, so much as the difference they make at various points in your life. How do I know that two people mean the same when each says he believes in God? And just the same goes for belief in the Trinity. A theology which insists on the use of *certain particular* words and phrases, and outlaws others, does not make anything clearer (Karl Barth). It gesticulates with words, as one might say, because it wants to say something and does not know how to express it. *Practice* gives the words their sense.

A proof of God's existence ought really to be something by means of which one could convince oneself that God exists. But I think that what *believers* who have furnished such proofs have wanted to do is give their 'belief' an intellectual analysis and foundation, although they themselves would never have come to believe as a result of such proofs. Perhaps one could 'convince someone that God exists' by means of a certain kind of upbringing, by shaping his life in such and such a way.

Das Leben kann zum Glauben an Gott erziehen. Und es sind auch *Erfahrungen*, die dies tun; aber nicht Visionen, oder sonstige Sinneserfahrungen, die uns die ›Existenz dieses Wesens‹ zeigen, sondern z. B. Leiden verschiedener Art. Und sie zeigen uns Gott nicht wie ein Sinneseindruck einen Gegenstand, noch lassen sie ihn *vermuten*. Erfahrungen, Gedanken, – das Leben kann uns diesen Begriff aufzwingen.

Er ist dann etwa ähnlich dem Begriff ›Gegenstand‹.

Ich kann Shakespeare darum nicht verstehen, weil ich in der gänzlichen Asymmetrie die Symmetrie finden will.

Mir kommt vor, seine Stücke seien, gleichsam, enorme *Skizzen*, nicht Gemälde; sie seien *hingeworfen*, von einem, der sich sozusagen *alles* erlauben kann. Und ich verstehe, wie man das bewundern und *es* die *höchste* Kunst nennen kann, aber ich mag es nicht. – Wer daher vor diesen Stücken sprachlos steht, den kann ich verstehen; wer sie aber bewundert, so wie man Beethoven etwa bewundert, der scheint mir Shakespeare mißzuverstehen.

Eine Zeit mißversteht die andere; und eine *kleine* Zeit mißversteht alle andern in ihrer eigenen häßlichen Weise.

Wie Gott den Menschen beurteilt, das kann man sich gar nicht vorstellen. Wenn er dabei wirklich die Stärke der Versuchung und die Schwäche der Natur in Anschlag bringt, wen kann er dann verurteilen? Wenn aber nicht, so ergibt eben die Resultierende dieser beiden Kräfte das Ziel, zu dem er prädestiniert wurde. Er wurde also geschaffen, um entweder durch das Zusammenspiel der Kräfte zu siegen, oder unterzugehen. Und das ist überhaupt kein religiöser Gedanke, sondern eher eine wissenschaftliche Hypothese.

Wenn Du also im Religiösen bleiben willst, mußt Du *kämpfen*.

Sieh Dir die Menschen an: Der eine ist Gift für den andern. Die Mutter für den Sohn, und umgekehrt, etc. etc. Aber die Mutter ist blind und der Sohn ist es auch. Vielleicht haben sie schlechtes Gewissen, aber was hilft ihnen das? Das Kind ist böse, aber niemand lehrt es anders sein, und die Eltern verderben es nur durch ihre dumme Zuneigung; und wie sollen sie es verstehen, und wie soll das Kind es verstehen? Sie sind sozusagen *alle* böse und *alle* unschuldig.

Die Philosophie hat keinen Fortschritt gemacht? – Wenn Einer kratzt, wo es ihn juckt, muß ein Fortschritt zu sehen sein? Ist es sonst kein echtes Kratzen,

Life can educate one to a belief in God. And *experiences* too are what bring this about; but I don't mean visions and other forms of sense experience which show us the 'existence of this being', but, e.g., sufferings of various sorts. These neither show us God in the way a sense impression shows us an object, nor do they give rise to *conjectures* about him. Experiences, thoughts, – life can force this concept on us.

So perhaps it is similar to the concept of 'object'.

The reason why I cannot understand Shakespeare is that I want to find symmetry in all this asymmetry.

His pieces give me an impression as of enormous *sketches* rather than of paintings; as though they had been *dashed off* by someone who can permit himself *anything*, so to speak. And I understand how someone can admire that and call *it supreme* art, but I don't like it. – So if someone stands in front of these pieces speechless, I can understand him; but anyone who admires them as one admires, say, Beethoven, seems to me to misunderstand Shakespeare.

One age misunderstands another; and a *petty* age misunderstands all the others in its own nasty way.

How God judges a man is something we cannot imagine at all. If he really takes strength of temptation and the frailty of nature into account, whom can he condemn? But otherwise the resultant of these two forces is simply the end for which the man was predestined. In that case he was created so that the interplay of forces would make him either conquer or succumb. And that is not a religious idea at all, but more like a scientific hypothesis.

So if you want to stay within the religious sphere you must *struggle*.

Look at human beings: one is poison to the other. A mother to her son, and vice versa, etc. But the mother is blind and so is her son. Perhaps they have guilty consciences, but what good does that do them? The child is wicked, but nobody teaches it to be any different and its parents spoil it with their stupid affection; and how are they supposed to understand this and how is their child supposed to understand it? It's as though they were *all* wicked and *all* innocent.

Philosophy hasn't made any progress? – If somebody scratches the spot where he has an itch, do we have to see some progress? Isn't it genuine scratching

oder kein echtes Jucken? Und kann nicht diese Reaktion auf die Reizung lange Zeit so weitergehen, ehe ein Mittel gegen das Jucken gefunden wird?

1951

Gott kann mir sagen: »Ich richte Dich aus Deinem eigenen Munde. Du hast Dich vor Ekel vor Deinen eigenen Handlungen geschüttelt, wenn Du sie an Andern gesehen hast.«

Ist der Sinn des Glaubens an den Teufel der, daß nicht alles, was als eine Eingebung zu uns kommt, von gutem ist?

Man kann sich nicht beurteilen, wenn man sich in den Kategorien nicht auskennt. (Freges Schreibart ist manchmal *groß;* Freud schreibt ausgezeichnet, und es ist ein Vergnügen, ihn zu lesen, aber er ist nie *groß* in seinem Schreiben.)[1]

---

[1] Vgl. *Zettel,* § 712.

otherwise, or genuine itching? And can't this reaction to an irritation continue in the same way for a long time before a cure for the itching is discovered?

1951

God may say to me: "I am judging you out of your own mouth. Your own actions have made you shudder with disgust when you have seen other people do them."

Is this the sense of belief in the Devil: that not everything that comes to us as an inspiration comes from what is good?

You cannot assess yourself properly if you are not well versed in the categories. (Frege's style of writing is sometimes *great*; Freud writes excellently and it is a pleasure to read him, but his writing is never *great*.)[1]

---

[1] Cf. *Zettel*, § 712.

SUBJECT INDEX

NAMENREGISTER/INDEX OF NAMES